Outback

The Jillaroo

ANNIE SEATON

The Augathella Girls: Book 4

ANNIE SEATON

This book is a work of fiction. Names, characters, places, magazines and incidents are the product of the author's imagination or are used fictitiously. Any resemblance to actual events, locales, or persons, living or dead, is coincidental.
Copyright © 2022 Annie Seaton

All rights reserved.

Dedication

For our four beautiful grandchildren:

Benny, Charlotte, Charlie and Georgia.

ANNIE SEATON

The Augathella Girls series.

Book 1: Outback Roads – The Nanny

Book 2: Outback Sky – The Pilot

Book 3: Outback Escape – The Sister

Book 4: Outback Winds – The Jillaroo

Book 5: Outback Dawn – The Visitor

Book 6: Outback Moonlight – The Rogue

Book 7: Outback Dust – The Drifter

Book 8: Outback Hope – The Farmer

Augathella Characters-Book 4

Amelia Foley	Jillaroo
Ben Riley	Shire Council Inspector
Sophie Cartwright	Station Cook
Kent Mason	Sophie's fiancé
Braden Cartwright	Sophie's brother
Callie Young	Braden's partner
Jon Ingram	Station Manager
Fallon Malone	Helicopter pilot
Jacinta Mason	Kent's sister
Harry Higgins	New doctor in town
Ruth Malone	Fallon's mother
Jenny Riley	Ben's mother

Chapter 1

Amelia

'That thing is a bloody danger!'

Amelia stared at the man who was glaring at Chilli Girl, her gentle golden retriever.

'It needs to be in a kennel or wear a muzzle.' His mouth was set in a straight line, and his tone was decidedly unfriendly. Normally Amelia wouldn't have flared up, but she'd just hung up on a call from her father and her mood had plummeted.

'Well, if you spoke to *him*—not *it*—properly and not just barged past, he—' she put her hands on her hips as Chilli crept behind her legs—'look, you've scared her.'

'So it's my fault your bloody dog bit me?' He frowned. 'He's a danger.'

'Chilli Girl's not a danger or a thing!' Amelia reached back and held onto Chilli Girl.

'Chilli Girl? I thought you said it was a he?'

'So if *it* was a he, or *she* was a he, she'd be more dangerous, and you'd be happy to yell at her?'

'What the—?'

The guy—who was starting to look familiar—and Amelia stood glaring at each other; her hand was on the scruff of Chilli's neck. If dogs could glare, Chilli was glaring at him too. Not that she'd hurt anyone, she was too gentle; she was just taking Amelia's side.

As she should.

Amelia lifted her chin, and Chilli gave a little whimper, sensing her mistress's mood. The mood that had more to do with her family than this guy. *He'd* just added to her day. She turned away from the cranky man and crouched down.

'It's okay, sweetie. Don't be sad. I'm fine. I'll be fine,' she murmured. 'No point letting two cranky men upset my day.' Amelia led Chilli to the gate of the new fence she'd put up, and gave her a gentle push. 'I put some treats in your bowl. Go and cheer up, I'll be fine.'

As she turned back to the man, he looked at her as though she was a complete ditz. That set a flame to the temper that had been simmering since Dad had demanded she come home this morning. He'd found her a job in Weipa, not far from their cattle station. A receptionist for the new solicitor who happened to be a friend of his.

'What?' she snapped. 'What are you looking at me like that for?'

He shook his head. 'I'm sorry. I don't mean to be rude, but you don't know if your dog is a dog or a bitch?'

'Don't call her a bitch. I hate that word. She's Chilli Girl, and she's a girl.'

'Okay, whatever she is, she needs controlling.'

'No, she doesn't. She didn't *bite* you, she was just being friendly. She liked you until you upset me and now if you want to get to know her, you'll have to win her back. She doesn't like people who speak to me like you just did.'

He pointed down to his work trousers. He looked totally out of place out here on the cattle station. Neatly creased trousers, a long-sleeved business shirt, a tie and a clipboard in his hand. '*She* ripped my trousers. Before I spoke to you.'

'I'll pay to replace them. She wasn't trying to hurt you; she wanted to play I've been on the phone and she was bored. Chilli's like a child. She needs stimulation, and she needs to play. I haven't had a chance to take her for a walk this morning. I'm sorry that she chose you as a potential playmate. You just happened to wander past at the wrong time. What are you doing anyway? It looks like you're working here, Mr—?' She widened her eyes as a thought came to her. 'You're not my new neighbour are, you? If you are, you'll have to make friends with Chilli Girl. I really hope you're not about to move in next door. You don't look like a ringer. No, you're not. You're a professional of some sort. The trousers, the long-sleeved shirt, the clipboard. Dead giveaway.' Amelia watched as his expression changed from disdain to mirth. 'Don't you dare laugh at me! It's disrespectful unless I've done something to amuse you.'

He chuckled again and her temper soared.

'I told you not to laugh at me.'

'I'm sorry. I'm not laughing at you. I'm laughing at the situation.' He smoothed his free hand down his perfectly pressed trousers—albeit with a *slight* tear—and then held it out to her. 'Let's start again. 'I'm Ben Riley and you're—?'

'I'm cross,' Amelia said, glancing to the left as she became aware of someone standing a short distance away from them

'Hi, Amelia,' Sophie said brightly, looking from one to the other with a quizzical expression on her face. 'I came down to ask you to the house for a drink, but it looks like you guys need to chill out a bit. How about you *both* come with me now, and we can have a beer or a wine? Ben, you've knocked off now, haven't you?'

He nodded. 'I have.'

'Well, both of you come up to the house and I'll tell Kent you're on the way. I think he'll be pleased to have a break from the boys. He's probably hiding from them.'

Sophie turned and headed back to the house.

Amelia looked at Ben for a long moment and took his outstretched hand. 'I guess you know my name now. I'm Amelia Foley and I won't say it's a pleasure to meet you. Yet.'

Chapter 2

Ben

Ben's cranky mood disappeared as quickly as the red dust from the willy willy that puffed along the fence behind them. 'I'm sorry you're still cross, and I'm sorry I was angry at your Chilli Girl. It's not been a good day for me. Let's take up Sophie's offer and start over.'

He was pleased when Amelia Foley reached over and shook his hand. And was surprised to feel the callouses on her small hand. She was petite and looked more suited to being at one of his mother's garden parties than bunking in a donga out in the bush. She was finely built and quite pretty. Dark hair, rosy cheeks—although they could be from the temper he'd caused. She didn't look like someone who would talk the leg off an iron pot, but once she started talking there was no stopping her.

Wide blue eyes held his. 'I'm Amelia Foley and now I know who you are. You played in the duo at that Easter concert.'

'I did.'

'So, what are you doing out here with a clipboard?' Her voice still held a slight tinge of anger, and her cheeks stayed that pretty rosy pink.

'Well, to answer your questions in order. No, I'm not your new neighbour. And I'm carrying a clipboard because I'm writing down the specs for the new dongas that Braden is going to build.'

'Why?'

'Because I'm an inspector at the local shire council, and I like what he's doing. I was interested to see them. I'm not inspecting or anything. There's no need to do that on a private station. He did ask me to check the concrete thickness, but that's a favour, not a council job.'

'Good.'

'Why good? That I'm not inspecting?'

'No. That you're not my neighbour.'

'No, I'm not. So, I guess you're still cross at me. I don't blame you.'

'Sort of. You wore my bad temper because I was already a bit out of sorts, but that's another story you don't want to hear. Okay, we'll start again. It *is* a pleasure to meet you, Ben Riley. I've forgiven you now, but you have to promise to be nice to Chilli Girl.'

'I can do that.' He nodded, but he wasn't going to let her get away with being rude to him 'And likewise, you're forgiven. Are you on a bush holiday? You're a long way from town. I didn't think Braden had started the holiday thing yet. He's been talking about it for a while.'

'No, I'm not on a holiday thing. I'm here for work.'

'Ah, you're the new nanny, now that Callie's working at the school.'

'No.'

'The cook?' He shook his head. He couldn't see her in the cookhouse. She looked like someone who should be sitting in a posh restaurant. Her voice was very cultured even when she was rabbiting on.

'No.'

'The housekeeper?'

'You're full of assumptions, aren't you, Ben Riley?'

'Sorry, you're hard to pick. I'm usually on the ball.'

'With women?'

He realised her hand was still in his and he let go. 'Hey, I'm not trying to come onto you or anything.'

'That's good because I wouldn't be interested if you were.'

His anger crept back in. 'Ditto. But I am going to ask you out for a coffee if you're in town, to apologise for my behaviour.'

He frowned.

Where the hell had that come from?

Her shoulders straightened and he was slightly offended when she laughed. 'No, thank you. I'm here to work, and besides, I don't know when I'll get to town again. It depends on what days Braden wants me to work.'

'Okay, what sort of work?'

'The cattle. I'm the new jillaroo.'

Surprise filled him again; that was the last thing he would have picked for her. It must have shown on his face as she put her hands on her hips.

'Sexist too, Ben Riley. Anyway, Sophie's waiting for us at the house. I'll meet you up there.' She turned away, but he reached out and held her arm, not wanting her to think he was a total arse, but the words that spilled out weren't what he'd intended. What was it about her that pushed his buttons? Delicate and dainty, but as strong as steel, she stared at him with her chin up.

'Hang on a minute. I haven't finished. In my role with the shire, I'm going to direct you to bring your dog, he, she or it, whatever, to the dog obedience classes in town.

'What? Why should I do that?'

'You don't want a dog bite complaint put in, do you?'

'You'd do that? You know, I really *don't* like you.'

'Yes, I'd do that.' He fought the grin that threatened as he looked at the determined expression on her face. 'For the safety of the

Augathella community.' The grin tugged harder as he looked at the docile golden retriever sitting there with a smile on *her* face.

She wouldn't agree to have coffee with him, but she could damn well come to town and he'd see her again.

Whether *she* liked it or not. If he had to stay in Augathella, he might as well enjoy himself.

Chapter 3

Amelia

As she and Ben approached the house—despite her instruction he go without her, *he* had waited—Amelia was surprised to see Kent, the other half of the singing duo, standing close to Sophie. From what Amelia had gathered the other day at the billy cart races, Kent and Sophie didn't get on. She'd even tried to give away the prize, she'd won. A date with Kent, the singer.

Now that Amelia had met the other half of the duo, she was pleased there hadn't been a raffle with the guitarist as the prize. She grinned; maybe they'd known they wouldn't sell many tickets for a date with a cranky man.

Sophie and Kent exchanged a glance as she and Ben came up the steps. Amelia was on one side of the wide stairs; Ben was on the other. She'd left Chilli in the fenced enclosure at the donga and Ben hadn't commented. In fact, they hadn't exchanged a word as they'd walked the hundred metres across to the main homestead.

Amelia had looked around with a satisfied sigh as they'd walked up. She hadn't had a chance to see much of the place so far, but she really liked what she could see.

The property wasn't as big as her family property up in the Gulf Country, but it was nowhere near as neat and tidy around the homestead as Dad insisted theirs was kept.

All the time. Not a blade of grass out of place. Not a recalcitrant drooping flower to be seen.

Then again, it made a difference when you could afford to employ a gardener just to maintain the house yard. A house yard that was almost a thousand kilometres from the nearest city and decent shops. Not to mention two and a half thousand kilometres to the boarding schools she and her five brothers had attended.

Despite the untidiness of the house yard, the unkempt garden, the swing set, and the bikes and toys scattered on the unmown grass held an appeal that was lacking at her family home. When she and the boys had been growing up—when they'd not been shipped off to boarding school, they had to keep their bikes neatly in the shed. She certainly couldn't imagine one of Mum's garden parties being held here, but the station had a warm welcoming feel.

It was a real *home*. A happy home. Amelia was sure she was going to be very happy working here for Braden Cartwright.

In fact, she was happy with everything here so far—except for the shire inspector. Sophie and Callie had welcomed her warmly, and Braden seemed like a really nice guy.

'Hi, guys. Grab a seat.' Kent smiled down at Sophie. 'I've just got to make a quick call and I'll bring some drinks out. Are you in a hurry, Ben?'

'No, not at all. How's the wrist?'

'Getting there. I'm actually coping a lot better.'

Envy ran through Amelia as she saw the way that Kent looked down at Sophie before he headed inside. Looked like they'd made up.

Amelia sat on the double sofa opposite the table and immediately regretted it when Ben smiled and sat beside her.

What was it with this guy?

One minute he was cranky and bossing her around, the next he was smiling at her and asking her out.

No way.

Amelia moved as close to her end of the soft seat as she could.

'Looking forward to starting work, Amelia?' Sophie sat on the chair across from them.

'I am. I was hoping to catch up with Braden and see what the schedule is. Is he around this afternoon?'

Sophie smiled, an air of suppressed excitement about her. 'Not at the moment. He and Callie had some important business to attend to. They should be back in an hour or two.'

'No matter. I'll see him in the morning. I'm getting myself organised.'

'So, a jillaroo, hey?' Ben said. 'A trainee station hand.'

Amelia raised her eyebrows. 'What's with the tone, Mr Inspector?'

Sophie's eyes widened.

'My *tone*?'

Amelia fought her rising temper as he kept talking.

'I guess I'm surprised that Braden's happy with a trainee when he has so much work on. Is this your first stint out of the city?'

'This is my first job in the west,' she answered. He didn't have to know she called herself a jillaroo because it sounded better than a ringer.

Bloody assumption-making rudeness. She really didn't like him. And she'd been honest enough to tell him that. No wonder Chilli Girl had bitten his trousers; she was an excellent judge of character.

Sophie stood. 'Okay, guys. Kent and I are babysitting. The boys have been playing hide and seek with him. They love hiding inside and goodness knows what sort of a mess they've made in there. Petie loves to get in the linen cupboard, but he pulls everything off the shelves before he climbs in, not knowing he's leaving a big clue in the hallway. I'll hunt them outside for a while.' Sophie disappeared through the door, and there was an uncomfortable silence between Amelia and Ben when they were left alone.

She cleared her throat and tried to think of something to say. He leaned back against the soft cushion, looking very much at ease.

Finally, she resorted to the weather. 'Looks like it hasn't rained out here for a while?'

'No.' The one-word answer didn't encourage that conversation to continue.

Stuff him. She could wait him out. He didn't know that she was used to dealing with five brothers who delighted in pushing her buttons. Silence was always a good strategy to keep control.

Amelia fought the chuckle that bubbled up. Her other strategy to feel comfortable with strangers was to talk non-stop until the other person interrupted. Mum had tried to teach her that wasn't ladylike, and that had made her do it all the more.

The silence was finally broken by pounding footsteps and happy yells as Braden's three boys ran out onto the wooden veranda.

They pulled up quickly when they saw they had company. Amelia was impressed with their manners as the tallest boy walked over.

'Hello, we saw you at the billy carts. Where's your dog?'

Ben gave her a look and she glared back at him before she turned to the boys.

'Hi there. Chilli's over having a snooze at our donga. Now let me see if I get your names right.' She put one finger to her lips. 'Rory, Nigel and—'

'I'm Petie, and it's really nice to see you again.' The littlest boy held his hand out and she took it with a smile.

'It's good to see you again, too, Petie. You have lovely manners.'

It was so good to have that uncomfortable silence broken.

'Callie taught me how to say that. I think she's going to be our new mum. I really, really hope so.'

'Ssh, Petie. Dad said we had to keep it a secret.' Rory lowered his voice. 'We're not allowed to say, but he's taken Callie to the range for the sunset and—'

'And he's going to ask her to be our new mum.' Rory obviously didn't want to be left out.

'Looks like we'll have to keep a secret,' Ben said.

'Hi Ben,' Rory said. 'Did you know we all have new dogs too? Callie said we might have to take them to your puppy school in Augathella to teach them some manners.'

'That sounds like a plan. What are their names?'

'Bumper, Tweedle and Apricot,' Nigel said.

'Great names, Nigel.' Amelia couldn't help her smile despite the new knowledge that Ben had something to do with the puppy school in town. She turned to look at Ben. 'Would that be the same school as the dog obedience school?'

He held her gaze steadily. 'It is, but Nigel, it's not my puppy school.'

'Can you come and watch if we come into town?'

'I can. I help out sometimes.'

Amelia raised her eyebrows as he glanced over at her, that damn sexy grin on his face again.

Gosh, where did that thought come from? She didn't even like the man.

'Amelia—is it okay if I call you that? —is going to bring her dog in too.' Ben glanced across at her again. He'd been doing that a lot since he'd sat beside her.

'Oh cool,' Nigel said. 'Would Chilli like to come and play with our pups now?'

Normally Amelia wouldn't have hesitated, but she was aware of Ben watching her. 'Maybe later. She's having a sleep now.'

'Okay, maybe we'll see her at the doggie school in town,' Nigel called over his shoulder as the three boys took off down the steps leaving her alone with Ben again.

Before the silence could become uncomfortable, Kent walked out juggling a tray with six glasses. Sophie was behind him, carrying a bottle of champagne.

'We're both really pleased to have you here with us to celebrate.'

'Callie and Braden's news?' Ben asked.

'No, our news. I asked Sophie to marry me and she said yes.' Kent beamed as he put his arm around Sophie. 'You guys are the first to know outside the family. We were waiting for Jacinta—my sister—to come home from Brisbane before we told anyone, but I just called her. We're really hoping it might be a double celebration tonight.'

Ben jumped up and hugged Sophie and then held out his hand to Kent. 'About bloody time, you two. We've all been waiting.'

Amelia stood too and came across to where the three friends were standing and gave them both a quick hug. 'Congratulations. Look, you don't want a stranger here. I'll head back to my donga and spend some time with Chilli.'

'Don't be silly.' Sophie shook her head. 'You won't do any such thing. This is going to be a party, and we'd love you to stay.'

'If you're sure?' Amelia said hesitantly.

'Absolutely,' Kent chimed in. 'Now take a seat while I get Ben to pop this cork. There are only so many things a man can do one-handed.'

The cork was popped and the fine crystal flutes filled with the effervescent liquid. When Sophie and Kent were settled on the other sofa, Ben raised his glass.

'To Sophie and Kent, may your wishes all come true.'

Amelia leaned forward and clinked her glass with the others. She watched Kent and Sophie as their engagement was toasted. The look on Kent's face as he held his fiancée's gaze was one that she hadn't seen very often. The only other time she'd seen it before was when Josh, her younger brother looked at his wife, Marnie. Sadly, Dad hadn't approved of him proposing to a station hand, and he'd given Josh an ultimatum.

The girl *or* his share in the property.

Amelia had been so proud of Josh when he'd chosen Marnie and they'd left *Granite Springs* and moved to Darwin.

Amelia hadn't had to make the choice, because being the only girl, she wouldn't get a share in the property, unless she married someone that Dad approved of. Frustration burned in her gut. She could be home working with the cattle on their spread, but to Dad, that was not a woman's role.

The last face-to-face fight she'd had with her father had seen her storming out, yelling at him. 'It's the twenty-first century, Dad. I don't know how the hell Mum's put up with you for thirty-five years.'

Today when he'd called had been the first contact she'd had with home since she'd left three months ago. And Dad hadn't changed his stance at all.

Pulling herself back to the happy moment here, she shook the thoughts of home and Dad away, and raised her glass. 'Nicely put, Ben. And yes, may all your wishes come true, Sophie and Kent. I'm really honoured to be a part of your day. I'll never forget it.'

'Thank you, Amelia. It's a very special day. It's been a long time coming, but we finally sorted ourselves out, didn't we, Kent?' Sophie looked across the yard as a white twin cab ute came up the road, slowed and turned in the gate. Excitement filled her voice. 'Oh look, here's Braden and Callie now. Oh please, please, I so hope she said yes.'

They all watched as the boys ran across to the vehicle when it pulled up outside the shed.

Amelia blinked back happy tears as Braden and Callie climbed out and held hands as they walked across to the boys.

Callie crouched down when they reached them and held her arms open. Braden stood there smiling.

'I guess she said yes,' Sophie said with a catch in her voice.

Chapter 4

Ben

'Another beer, Ben?' Braden's smile hadn't left his face since he and Callie had joined them. There'd been another round of congratulations, and then Ben had had a couple of beers.

Ben got a shock when he looked at his watch 'Geez, it's almost nine. If I have one more, I'll have to bunk here in my swag if that's okay.'

'Sure is. Did you say nine? I didn't realise how late it was. I'll light the barbie and throw some steaks on.'

'It's a wonder the boys haven't been out looking for dinner. I've been slack.' Callie stood. 'I'll get them sorted and then throw a salad together.'

'Don't worry too much, love. Let's do burgers. Does that suit everyone?' Braden stood beside Callie and put his arm around her waist. 'Kent and Soph, you're welcome to stay the night.'

'We will,' Kent agreed.

Ben nodded as well. 'Thanks, mate, I will too. I'll give you a hand to cook.' He looked over at Amelia; she was curled up in the corner of the sofa, her legs tucked beneath her. Looking up, she caught his eyes on her, and a faint tinge of pink coloured her cheeks again. She uncurled her legs and sat up.

'Can I help you in the kitchen, Callie?' She looked away from Ben.

'Thanks, Amelia. I'll get you chopping some onions. Sophie hates doing that.'

'I sure do. I'll get some tomato, lettuce and beetroot going. Burgers sound good to me. Can we have eggs on them too? I'm starving.'

'You're always starving, Sophie,' Braden teased.

'Runs in the family, big brother, and those three boys are the same. You must miss me now that I've moved over to Kent's.'

'Callie and I manage, don't we, love?'

'We do.' Callie reached up and kissed Braden's cheek.

'Do you need some buns out of the freezer? Won't take long to thaw,' Sophie asked as she stood.

'Yes, please,' Callie said.

'Come and help me, Kent.' Sophie tugged him up by his good hand. 'You should be able to manage one bag.'

'I'm not that incapacitated,' he replied, nudging her shoulder.

By nine-thirty, the steaks and eggs had been cooked, the smell of frying onions filled the air, and a long table had been set up in the breezeway.

Ben sat opposite Amelia, as the two newly-engaged couples naturally paired up. Rory, Nigel and Petie had apparently taken care of their own dinner.

'I can't be cross. They've all crashed in their bean bags in front of the television.' Callie had come out of the kitchen with her hands on her hips. 'While we were out here drinking champagne, they raided the kitchen. It won't hurt them to have Tim Tams and potato chips for dinner one night, will it?

Sophie laughed. 'No, it won't. They were celebrating too.'

Braden had gone inside and helped Callie put the boys to bed while Kent and Ben manned the barbeque.

'Bet you didn't do this in Charters Towers,' Kent said to him as Ben flipped the steaks over.

'Only because I didn't know many people there. But I will give you that. There's nothing like country hospitality. I did miss it when I was there.'

'Yet, you're breaking your neck to get out of here. Can't understand you, mate, but each to his own.'

'Yeah. I couldn't believe it when I got seconded back to Morweh Shire. They thought they were doing me a favour sending me home.'

'They were. Who'd want to live anywhere else?'

'Me,' Ben replied.

'If you had your own place and weren't living with your olds, you might find it better.'

'Maybe.' Ben shrugged. He'd had that thought himself but he didn't want to buy his own place until he was sure where he wanted to settle. At the moment, that place wasn't Augathella.

Kent sent him a sideways look. 'Is there someone special up north? Have you left your heart there?'

'Hell, no. I'm going to stay a free agent until I'm forty. I'll think about a wife and kids then. By that time, I'll know where I want to live.'

'Famous last words, mate. I saw the way you were sussing out the new ringer. She's a looker.'

'That may be, but she's not my type.'

'Why's that?'

'She's sassy and bossy and hang on . . . did you say ringer? I thought she was a trainee jillaroo.'

'No, she's really experienced. She comes from one of the biggest stations up in the Gulf.'

'Really? She looks more like a city girl.'

'I saw you checking her out a few times tonight.'

'She sure led me on. Don't you tell her I know where she's from. I'll hold that one up my sleeve. And don't go trying to set us up.' He wasn't going to tell Kent that he'd asked her out already, and been knocked back.

Amelia's rejection had stung, but to be fair they hadn't got off on the right foot. He had to admit she was a very attractive woman, and maybe they *could* spend some time together, but her expression had shown she wasn't interested.

More than once.

And if there was one thing Ben knew, he wouldn't be pushing.

He wouldn't.

Chapter 5

Amelia

Amelia woke just after dawn as she always did. Not because it was getting light, but because Chilli Girl was making the usual "time to wake up" noises to let her know it was time to go for a walk. Amelia slipped on a pair of jeans and a hoodie over the T-shirt she'd slept in. After gathering up a doggie-disposal bag out of habit, and her phone, she slipped on a warm pair of socks and her boots. By the time she opened the door, the first fingers of sunlight were shining on the hills to the west.

She'd go for a long walk, and with any luck, Ben Riley would be gone by the time she ventured down to the homestead to have the meeting she and Braden had organised last night.

It would be interesting checking out the paddocks, she'd noticed a few cattle not far from the house yard last night before it got dark. As she stepped onto the front porch, she caught a glint of sunlight in the distance. A large expanse of water sparkled in the early sunlight.

'Good morning, Chilli Girl. Were you warm enough out here last night?' Amelia crouched down and dropped a kiss on Chilli's nose, before clipping the lead to her collar 'I can see some water. We're going to go for a long walk, and then have some breakfast.'

Even though Braden had said it was okay for Chilli to go inside the donga, Amelia hadn't thought it was the right thing to do. He'd been good enough to let her bring Chilli to a working station. If it got too cold at night, Chilli could sleep in her van at night.

They set off across the first paddock, and Amelia admired the sleek and shiny cattle in the distance. It was a glorious morning, with the promise of warmth already. Even though she'd grown up in the Gulf Country, she was well used to the cold after her ten years of boarding school in Toowoomba.

The dam was further away than she'd thought and by the time they reached it, the sun was high in the sky and she'd removed her hoodie. The dam covered a couple of acres and the paddocks around were obviously irrigated. The grass was green and lush, so different from the dry tussocky grass of the Gulf. Contentment settled over Amelia; Braden had said that the contract here was a long one if they were both happy with her first week. This morning, they'd discuss her work.

'Oops, Chilli, we'd better get a move on. I can't be late to meet the boss!'

##

An hour later Amelia had fed Chilli, eaten a quick bowl of muesli and dressed neatly in good jeans and button-up collared shirt. She reached for her clean boots and gave them a quick wipe-over with her socks.

'Now you stay here and behave. I won't be long.' As Amelia gave the instructions to Chilli, she wondered whether she had made a mistake bringing her out to the station. When they'd been travelling, she'd been no trouble at all; she was a well-behaved dog who never barked or showed any aggression.

The incident yesterday afternoon with Ben Riley had rattled Amelia. Not that she thought Chilli would have hurt him—or anyone—but the fact that she'd be out working long days on the station would mean she'd be left in the small fenced area for hours at a time, and it wasn't really fair to leave Chilli unattended.

Biting her lip as she strode along the road towards the homestead, she worried about Chilli. Maybe she'd have to see if she could have her boarded in town the days she was working. She shook her head with a frown; she really hadn't thought this out well. The road out here had almost finished her two-wheel-drive van, and the thought of driving in and out of town every week didn't appeal. She could almost hear her dad talking to her. 'So typical of you, Amelia. Just plunge into things without thinking about it.'

That was unfair because she usually *did* think things through. She'd picked up Chilli, a rescue dog, on the spur of the moment a few months ago because she was lonely. Such a cute little pup, and she'd quickly grown into a lovely young dog. All the more reason to think about buying her own place and settling.

Maybe land close to Augathella wasn't too expensive. A small holding would do her, big enough to run a few cattle, have enough room for her horse, Brinny, and maybe grow some vegies and have some chooks. She didn't need a big flash house or shed. It would be fun to do an old place up, a home that would be hers and Chilli's.

Finance wasn't a problem, thanks to an inheritance from her beloved Grandma—her mother's mother who knew that Dad wasn't going to give his only daughter any share in the family property.

I don't care. Amelia was determined to make her own way in life, even if it was with a little help from Gran.

As she drew closer to the homestead her mood plummeted further as she saw Ben Riley walking out towards his ute. She'd hoped he'd be long gone by now.

'Good morning, Amelia.' His smile was wide and she forced one back. Last night, she'd warmed to him a bit, but she was still wary.

'You're looking very swish this morning,' he said.

Amelia scowled. 'Would you say the same thing to Braden or Kent?'

He frowned as he swung a swag onto the back of his ute. 'Get out of the wrong side of the bed this morning, did you? Or are you hungover?'

'No, to both.' Amelia glared at him. 'You're looking a little seedy yourself. You put away a few beers last night.'

'Were you counting?' he asked. 'I'm flattered that you take such an interest in my well-being.'

'No. I wasn't.' She wished she'd merely nodded at him and kept walking. Not even her brothers got her this cranky. She forced a sweet smile to her face. 'I have a meeting with Braden. You have a lovely day, Mr Riley.'

'Oh, I intend to. I hope you do too, Ms Foley.' He reached into his shirt pocket as he walked over to her. 'Here's the details for the puppy school.'

Her eyes widened. 'Puppy school?' She bit back the rude answer that sprang to her lips.

'Yes, remember? Before I knocked off last night and we became social acquaintances, I directed you to bring Chilli Girl to the dog obedience classes in town.'

'Are you for real?'

'Yes, I certainly am. To avoid any more dangerous confrontations with the public, I directed you to bring her to the classes. Take the card and call. My mother will fit you in.'

She took the card from him and put it carefully in her shirt pocket. 'I thought that would normally be a ranger role?'

He nodded. 'Yes, it is, however, we are a small shire and we share the load. I'll see you in town.'

Without another word—or direction—he climbed into the ute and drove out towards the gate.

Amelia was thoughtful as she approached the house. Was he serious, or was he having a lend of her? She could have sworn a smile was playing around his mouth as he'd been "directing" her.

Braden came out of the house as she walked up the steps. 'Morning, Amelia. I hope you slept well. We had a pretty late night, didn't we? Have you had breakfast?'

'I have, thank you. I've been for a walk out to the dam too.'

'Great. I ate with Ben. Kent and Sophie left early, and Callie's taken the three boys to school. Did you know she works in there as a teacher three days a week?'

'No, I didn't.'

'Come on, we'll go over to my office in the big shed. I'm looking forward to hearing more about what you prefer to do. We've got a few different areas that I need filled.'

'Great, I'm looking forward to working here.'

Amelia's mood lifted. Everything was going to be fine.

Chapter 6

Ben

Ben sang along with the radio as he drove back to town. He was heading home to have a quick shower and shave, and change into some clean work clothes before he headed into the shire office. Being Friday, there was a staff muster at nine-thirty to wrap up the week.

It was one of the newly-elected mayor's communication strategies, and the mayor drove out to both Augathella and Morven offices to attend the meetings each week. The communication in the shire was top notch and it was one of the happiest workplaces Ben had worked in over the past few years. Shame it was where he didn't want to be.

Although last night had been fun. It had been great catching up with friends and seeing them so happy.

It had been one of those off-the-cuff occasions that usually turned into the best nights. Seeing Kent and Sophie engaged and living together now, had been great. Kent had been bloody miserable at the fundraising gig they did at Craig Wilson's place at Easter.

Seeing Braden happy, and his boys back to their normal boisterous selves had been really good too. Ben had been living in Longreach when Julia had been killed, and when Kent and Sophie had broken up around the same time, but he had no doubt about the grief and unhappiness that had touched *Kilcoy Station* since then. Mum had kept him up to date, and she'd gone to Julia's funeral. Ben had made the effort to catch up with Braden as soon as he'd arrived back in town.

Callie seemed like a good person, and the boys loved her, from what he'd seen last night.

And then there was Amelia Foley. As much as he hated to admit it, Ben was very keen to see her again. Even this morning, when she'd been on the way to her meeting and was cold as ice to him, he'd not been able to stop looking at her. It wasn't just her looks; there was something about her that fascinated him.

Last night as they'd celebrated the two engagements, he'd caught himself watching her a few times.

He knew he'd been pushy about the dog obedience class, but he hoped that was a ruse that would get her to town. Either that, or it would turn her off him for life.

Either way, it didn't matter. He was on the lookout for a new job; a job far away from

Augathella where he'd grown up. So, if she did agree to go out with him, it would only be a casual date.

No strings attached.

His mother's Audi was in the drive as he pulled up outside the sprawling weatherboard house where he'd spent his childhood. As Ben opened the front gate, a small silver bullet shot off the veranda and raced down the path.

'Hey, Albie boy, watcha doin'?' He bent down and gave in to the exuberant licks all over his face and neck from his mother's little dog.

'Hi, darling. Did you have a nice night?' His mother came around the side of the house, garden hose in hand.

'Morning, Mum. And yes, I did.'

He'd called from Braden's to let Mum know he wouldn't be home last night. Another black mark against living in Augathella. Christ, he was almost thirty-two years old, and he was ringing his parents to report in. Too bad if he'd wanted to bring someone home after a hot date. The only other alternative was a room at the pub, and if he did that it would spread around the town like wildfire.

Nope, he was out of here.

Which reminded him that he hadn't checked the online job site for a few days. That would be his first task this morning after the muster at the council office.

The other thing he'd maybe have a look at was the land for sale around the district. That was another alternative. He was starting to like this job on the shire; it was living at home and feeling like a teenager that was doing his head in.

'Let me cook you some bacon and eggs. Have you got time before you go to work?'

'Thanks, Mum. I had a feed with Braden.'

'Okay, I'll just make a pot of tea for us, then.'

'I really don't have time. I just came home for a quick shower and shave. I've got a meeting.'

'All right. You go and jump in the shower and I'll get your clothes out for you. I'll still make a cuppa in case you feel like one after your shower.'

Ben gritted his teeth and raced up the steps and into the bathroom. There was no point objecting. Even if he told Mum not to do it, his clothes would still be laid out on his bed. The same bed he'd had since he was ten years old.

No wonder Dad went away so much. He spent most of his time working on remote properties.

As Ben dried off and shaved after a quick shower, guilt trickled through him. Mum was lonely, and she'd always wanted to be needed. He walked into his room, and sure enough, a neatly pressed pair of clean trousers and his favourite shirt were laid out on the bed.

He dressed quickly and hurried into the kitchen where she was sitting at the table, a pot of tea and two mugs in front of her.

'Just a quick one, Mum,' he said, feeling sorry for her. 'I've got a meeting soon.' He dropped a kiss on the top of her head and she smiled up at him. 'What have you got planned for today?'

Kent poured a mug of tea, and Mum pushed over the sugar basin and a teaspoon.

'Not a lot, love. A bit of gardening, a load of washing, and I'll take Albie for a walk later. What would you like for dinner?'

'Don't bother, I'll sort something.' Ben hated committing to being home for dinner each night. 'Oh, and while I think of it, Mum, I gave out one of your cards today. If an Amelia rings, can you book her in as early as you can?'

'Amelia? Is she new in town?'

'She's working out at Kilcoy Station. She's got a lovely golden retriever, but she's a bit naughty.'

'Amelia is?'

Ben chuckled. 'No, her dog. Chilli Girl. I've got a tear in the trousers I chucked in the laundry basket. Anyway, I suggested that she brings her into puppy school.'

'Thanks, darling. It's been quiet these last couple of weeks. Everyone's been busy with Easter and the school holidays.'

'Dad still coming home next weekend?'

His mother's face lit up in a wide smile. 'Yes, and he'll be home for two whole weeks.'

Kent nodded. 'Sounds good. I'm heading up to Tambo the weekend after next, so you'll have some time to yourselves. Kent and I have a gig at the pub.'

'I'm so proud of you. You were both so good out at the Wilson's place. Aren't you pleased I made you take those guitar lessons after school?'

'I am, Mum. But I have to get going now. Not sure if I'll be in for dinner tonight, so please don't worry about cooking for me.'

He grabbed his keys and headed for the back door.

'I'll cook you something just in case and leave it in the fridge.'

Ben sighed as he headed out to the ute.

Mum meant well, but she was doing his head in.

Chapter 7

Amelia

After spending an hour with Braden, and discussing what he expected, Amelia was on top of the world. Jon Ingram, the station manager had arrived halfway through their meeting, and joined them for a coffee.

Braden needed her for cattle work, but he was mainly looking for someone who specialised in the health of the beasts. And that was right up her alley.

'You know,' he'd said. The sort of things you don't need to trouble the local vet for. And poor Jed McAdam is run off his feet. He can't get anyone to move out here and work his practice with him. We get to know our herd, and we know the problems we face, so if we can handle most of it out in the paddocks, that saves us time and money.'

Jon nodded. 'With the experience you've had, Amelia, that will save us heaps of time. I'll take you out on horseback next week to the steers that are close in and you can see what we mean. When we go way out, we'll camp out. I guess you've got a swag and a groundsheet?'

Amelia nodded, but she hesitated before she spoke.

Braden interrupted. 'I know exactly what you're worried about, but don't worry. When you're working out overnight, Chilli can go in the pen with the boys' three dogs. That is if you're happy with that?'

Amelia could have kissed him. 'Really? Are you sure that's not a huge inconvenience? I was going to try and get her boarded in town.'

Braden chuckled. 'I'm sure Ben would have looked after her for you. He puts on a tough front, but he's always been a softie when it comes to dogs. His mum used to work at the vet after she retired as a teacher, and now she has the puppy preschool.'

'No. I wouldn't trouble him, but if you're sure she'll be fine here. . .'

'Of course, she will. That dog enclosure is safe, and it's got more toys than the three boys combined. It's teaching the boys some responsibility, and with a grown pup to look after, it'll be another lesson.'

'What sort of dog have you got?' Jon asked as he reached for the coffee mug and one of the chocolate biscuits Braden had brought out.

'She's a pure-bred golden retriever,' Amelia answered, trying to ignore the temptation of the biscuits. 'She's just over a year old, so she's over most of the puppy chewing stage. She was abandoned in one of the small towns I travelled through and when they couldn't find an owner, I volunteered to take her. We've been great mates ever since. And she's never any trouble. Usually.' She glanced at Braden.

He laughed. 'Jon, she took a dislike to Ben Riley. He was wandering around near the dongas measuring the new concrete floors for me. She went for him.'

Amelia shook her head. 'She didn't actually bite him. She was playing and she tore his trousers. He flared up and he took it the wrong way. She wants to be everyone's friend.'

'Anyway, she's welcome to stay in the run with the other three whenever you have to head out. We do have some late nights here.'

Jon put his cup down. 'Are you more comfortable on horseback or bike? We've got a couple of all-terrain four-wheelers too.' He glanced nervously at Braden, but he was checking a message on his phone.

'Either or,' Amelia said. 'I'm experienced, and comfortable on both, and I'm a competent horsewoman.'

'We use helicopters to muster, and sometimes to survey the livestock and the watering points that are way out. Any questions?'

'No all good. I'm looking forward to getting to work. Tomorrow?'

Braden looked up and shook his head. 'Monday. That way you can go into town with Callie and the boys for the dog obedience class.' He held her gaze, and Amelia's mouth dropped open but she shut it before any argument could come out.

She swallowed and then nodded. 'Okay, that sounds like a plan. Thanks again.'

'I'll just finish up here with Braden and I'll meet you over at the shed near the horse paddock,' Jon said. 'Do you know where that is?'

'I do.'

'Okay, give me about twenty minutes and we'll saddle up for an hour or two.' He frowned. 'As long as that's okay with you.'

'Suits me fine. It'll be great to be on horseback. It's been a few weeks.' Amelia stood and pushed the chair in. 'I took a bit of a break on the way down from the Gulf.'

As she walked out, she wondered why Braden was so keen to get her and Chilli into those dog obedience classes. It sort of felt like a setup but she couldn't object, because he'd been so good with letting her bring Chilli to the station, and then the offer to let her stay with the three other pet dogs when she was working had been so unexpected.

She'd appreciated his kindness, what was one afternoon in town at a dog obedience class?

***

Braden waited until Amelia was out of earshot. 'So, you think she'll work out?'

'If she's anything like her brothers and her father, you'll want to hang onto her.'

'You know them?' Braden raised his eyebrows.

'I worked on Granite Springs for a few months a couple of years ago.'

'Amelia didn't remember you?'

Jon shook his head as he reached for the coffee pot. 'She was away when I was there. Overseas, I think. But she has a reputation as a formidable horsewoman.' He chuckled. 'Apparently, she has no fear, and is as tough as they come.'

'You sure wouldn't get that from looking at her.'

'Don't let appearances deceive you, Braden, although I know what you mean. I'll never forget the first time Fallon took me up in the chopper, and I misjudged her. Amelia's a tiny thing, but according to her brothers, she swears like a trooper and can outride any of them. She has the look of her father, but by God, he was a tough boss. Not popular with the stock manager or any of the ringers, or to be honest, his boys. If she's as feisty as they say, I can imagine she would have clashed with Greg Foley.'

'Interesting. I like her. She joined in with our celebration last night. Ben Riley was here too.'

'Celebration?' Jon looked curiously at his boss.

'Callie's agreed to marry me. And Kent and Sophie got engaged too.'

Jon stood and held out his hand to Braden. 'Congratulations, mate. That's great news. I'm happy for you.'

Braden shook his hand and grinned at him. 'Thanks, mate. I think Callie was going to ring Fallon today and tell her. We're having a bit of a formal do in town in a couple of weeks. Would love to see you there. How is Fallon? Keeping well?'

'She is, but she's sick of herself. The doc's sending her to Charleville for another scan next week.' Jon shook his head. 'He suspects twins.'

'Holy hell, that's pretty special.'

Jon nodded. 'Pretty scary. I would think one's enough of a challenge.'

'Mate, trust me. An old hand here. You'll be fine. After a few days, it's just like you've always had a kid.' He lowered his voice. 'I'd like to think Callie and I will have kids.'

'We could almost start our own school out here.' Jon started to walk to the door. 'That reminds me. What's the go with Amelia's dog and puppy school? Is it a terror?'

'No, Chilli's a great dog.' Braden's grin was wide. 'I'm just helping a mate along. There was a definite spark between Amelia and Ben last night, but she put some barriers up. I'm—'

'You're playing matchmaker.'

'Possibly. Are you heading into town this afternoon?'

'Yeah, Fallon's got an appointment with the new doctor.'

'New doctor? What happened to Doc Henry? He's not crook, is he?'

'No, but he doesn't want to do the commute from Charleville anymore, so the board advertised and appointed a new doc last week. Harry Higgins. Seems like a nice enough bloke. Bit quiet, but came with a great reputation.'

'Wife and kids?'

'Nah, came by himself from all accounts.'

'I'll have to drop in and say gidday. Listen, while you're in town, do me a favour?'

'What's that, mate?'

'If you see Ben, tell him to give his mother a night off from the puppy school. He'll understand why.'

'You really are matchmaking. I'm glad I'm settled now. You're a bad man, Braden Cartwright.'

'Just like to see everyone happy.'

It's good to see you happy, mate.' Jon thumped him on the arm on the way out.

Chapter 8
Friday afternoon
Amelia

Amelia sat in the front with Callie, the four dogs were tied up and lying on a blanket on the back seat. They were remarkably quiet and when Amelia glanced over the back, she could see that Chilli had gone to sleep.

'It's a big day for the boys. I don't work Fridays so Braden drives them to school,' Callie said. 'Petie does half a day at kindy and then Fallon's mum picks him up. The other two go to her place after school and stay there until I go in and get them. Ruth adores them. She's going to make a fabulous granny.'

Amelia knew she must have looked blank when Callie hurried on with an explanation.

'You probably don't know Fallon?'

Amelia shook her head.

'She's Jon's fiancée. They're having their first bub in about three months. Fallon came to town about the same time Jon came back to the district to work with Braden. I'd been here a couple of weeks, and I was still feeling my way around. Fallon and I hit it off and we've become good friends. Her mum and dad came to town when they discovered they were going to be grandparents.'

'Where from?' Amelia asked. She couldn't imagine her mum and dad following her to Augathella. She hid a smile as Callie answered.

'Brisbane. But there's some family connection. They're cleaning out an old uncle's house ready to put on the market.'

Amelia's interest quickened. 'Any land around it?'

'A few acres I think.'

'Is it in town?'

'Just on the edge, I think. Why? Are you looking for a place?'

'If the right place came up, maybe. But I want to suss out the area first. I love the thought of working on Kilcoy Station, but I haven't seen much of town yet. When I first hit Augathella at Easter, it was packed, and I'm guessing that's unusual.'

Callie shook her head. 'I've been surprised how many tourists come out this way. There's always something happening in one of the towns. The new shire mayor is a real dynamo, and he's getting all the towns connected. Charleville, Morven, Augathella and Cooladdi. He even does a Facebook video every week to let the shire know what's going on. I thought I was coming out to the sticks to a sleepy country town, but there's more to do here than I ever did in Brisbane.' She grinned at Amelia. 'Who ever would have guessed I'd be happy living in the remote outback? My friends in Brisbane can't believe it, and they're sending Jen, my best friend, out here to make sure I'm not off my rocker. If anyone had told me six months ago I'd be driving along a dirt outback road with four dogs in the back and heading to a little town to go to puppy school, I would have thought they were mad.'

'So, tell me how you got out here, Callie. Why does everyone think you're mad? Did you meet Braden when you were out here on holidays? Or did you meet him in Brisbane?'

'It's a long story, Amelia.'

'I love a good story. But if you'd prefer not to share. . .'

'No, it's okay. It took a while but I'm fine about it now. Being out here in the wide-open spaces makes some things seem trivial. In the city, everything seems magnified. Out here, you know what matters. And when I met Braden and the boys and realised what they'd been through—his wife died in an accident in a storm.'

'Oh, how sad. Such little boys.'

'Yes, adorable little boys who are coping remarkably well these days. Sophie was a godsend for Braden, and when she went away, he advertised for a nanny.'

'And you applied?'

'I was looking for a job, any job, as long as I got as far away from Brisbane as I could.'

'That doesn't sound good.'

'Actually, it was my own fault. I was sort of engaged to this guy I worked with.'

'Sort of?'

'Yes, I was too trusting. I was a presenter on the weather channel at one at the networks in Brisbane. Unbeknown to me, he was doing the dirty behind my back and naive me thought we were about to get engaged no matter what his excuses were. I was after a stable relationship. He was after my property and investments.'

'Oh, no!'

Callie nodded and rolled her eyes. 'To cut a long story short he proposed to his other woman on national television. I saw red and I didn't realise the cameras were still rolling. I went over and shoved him on his bum. And it was seen by millions of viewers.'

'Sounds like he got everything he deserved.'

'That may be the case, but it went viral on TikTok and I was absolutely mortified. So, I went looking for a job as a school teacher—I trained and worked as a teacher for a few years before I met Greg. But I'll be forever grateful that I found the nanny job out at Kilcoy Station.' She took her eyes off the road for a second and glanced at Amelia.

'And here I am six months later, engaged to Braden and about to become a step mum. Three gorgeous little boys who I already adore. So that's enough about me. Tell me how you ended up at Augathella.' She smiled and gestured over to the backseat. 'I mean how did you and Chilli Girl end up at Augathella?'

Chilli heard her name and gave a soft woof from the back seat. Amelia turned around, reached out and gave her a quick pat. 'Nearly there. You've been such a good girl.' She turned back around in her seat. 'My story's not as exciting as yours. I grew up on the Gulf of Carpentaria on a cattle station.'

'So, you're a genuine outback girl.'

'Not really. I haven't spent a lot of time there since I was about ten.'

'How come? Is it still your home?' Callie slowed as an emu appeared in the paddock on the passenger side.

'It is, but my father doesn't believe women should have a place out on the land, but ever since I was a little girl, I've loved station life. The cattle, the horses, outback life. He did everything he could to turn me into a lady.'

'I think you're very ladylike,' Callie said as she sped up again.

'My mum was the same too. Mum is so old school she still gets changed and puts makeup on before Dad comes in from the station in the afternoon.' Amelia rolled her eyes as she thought of home. 'Would you believe she even hosts garden parties in the middle of nowhere?'

'Who for?' Callie frowned. 'If you are so isolated, I mean.'

'Oh, it's a weekend event for the Gulf Country. Every spring, the Foley garden party is an event not to be missed. Families fly and drive in. Hundreds of kilometres.'

'Wow, sounds pretty special.'

Amelia shook her head. 'Not really. I don't think Mum's even aware that most people in the twenty-first century don't even know what a garden party is.'

'Actually, I do.' Callie flicked her a glance. 'There's a garden party in Augathella the weekend after next. Ben's mum apparently has one in autumn and spring each year.'

'Save me,' Amelia said, but she smiled. 'Anyway, to cut a long story short I didn't fit in as the daughter they wanted. I was sent to boarding school, then secretarial college, and when finishing school in Switzerland was discussed, I bailed. Dad wouldn't let me work on the place, even though I am more than capable. He thought my five brothers were enough. Although there's only four there now because Josh, my younger brother, and Dad didn't get on, but that's another story.'

'So, you set off to find your own way?'

'I did. I packed up and travelled around for a little while and came across my Chilli Girl up near Longreach. I needed the company, and she was there, and then a few months after travelling the west, I saw the job advertised here at Kilcoy Station.'

'And we're glad you did. I think you'll fit right in, Amelia. This place gets into your heart. The locals are lovely, and there's so much to do.'

'So far, I love everything. Everyone I've met has been so welcoming. Even the old guy I met at the pub at Augathella when I was watching the billy cart races before I met you guys was fun. We had a lovely chat about the age of the artesian bore water. I must follow him up when I'm in town and see if he looked it up on Google.'

Callie chuckled. 'Old Reg is a town institution. You won't have any trouble finding him if you do go looking. Always at the same table outside the pub, day in, day out.'

'I'll make sure I go and talk to him again.'

'That's sweet of you. You'll do well here, Amelia. It's great to have you in Augathella.'

As they approached the turnoff into town, Callie slowed and put the indicator on. 'Are you and Chilli ready for puppy school?'

'We are.'

'We'll call in and pick the boys up at Ruth's place. It'll give you a chance to have a look at the property if you really are interested. I know it's coming on the market soon. Then I'll drop you and the three boys at puppy school. I'm going to go to school and do some photocopying for my lessons tomorrow.'

'Puppy school,' Amelia echoed. 'Why do I have a bad feeling about this?'

***

Ben jumped as a squeal came from behind him in the hallway.

'Gawd, Mum, you frightened ten years growth out of me with that squeal. What's wrong?'

'*You* scared me! I didn't know you were home, love. I didn't see your car out the front. I would have got some afternoon tea ready for you if I'd known you were coming home early. I was watering the back garden and didn't hear your car. Have you got a gig with Kent tonight?'

'No, I came home early because I'm running an extra puppy school class tonight, I meant to tell you. Did anyone ring?'

'No, she didn't.' His mother frowned. 'An extra one? An extra class? What for? We've never done that before.'

'Ah . . . um . . . the Cartwright boys have got three new dogs and I thought it would be good to have them all together by themselves rather than mixed in with the usual whole class. Plus, there's a new girl out there at Kilcoy Station and she's got a golden retriever that needs a bit of work, so I offered for them to come in together this afternoon.'

Mum raised her eyebrows, and a smile twitched at her lips. 'And you've showered and shaved. Is there something you're not telling me? You *never* shave in the afternoon, Benny boy.'

'Like what?' Ben reached for another towel and rubbed his hair. 'Tell you what?'

'I don't know. I thought you were busy at work. And I didn't think you wanted to have much to do with the obedience school anymore.'

'Well, to be honest, the girl out there who has the dog, she went for me.'

'The girl?'

'No, the retriever. I told her in my role as shire inspector that she had to come to obedience school.'

'You told the dog?'

'No, Mum.' Ben tried to keep his voice patient. He knew when his mother was trying to wind him up and he wasn't going to bite. 'I told the *owner* that the dog would have to come to obedience school.'

'What? You can't do that. You're the shire inspector, not the shire ranger.'

'Okay. But if you do happen to meet her, her name is Amelia and please don't mention that.'

'Mention what?'

'My role. My job. What I do.'

His mother frowned. 'I suppose it's a bit of a worry if the retriever is dangerous, around the little kids out there at Kilcoy. Is it a rescue dog? Maybe it—did you say Chilli Girl? Maybe she has a problem with men? You never know where rescue dogs have been and what treatment they've had. Remember that little rescue Maltese Terrier that come through here with those grey nomies last year? She hated little girls.'

'No, Mum, I wasn't here last year. Remember?'

His mother waved her hand, still encased in a gardening glove. 'Well, whatever. You know what I mean. A lot of them have problems, and we have to work extra hard with them. They're all redeemable, poor little pets. It's not their fault.'

'Well, Chilli's not exactly dangerous. I think she was just protecting her owner. I gave them both a fright when I came around the side of the building.'

A slow smile spread across his mother's face. 'Hmm. So, there's another side to the story, my lad, is there? I'm guessing this Amelia is a pretty young lady.'

'Yeah, she's okay.' Ben tried to sound nonchalant. 'Not bad.'

'Ben, I know you well. There's no reason why you would ever run an extra puppy school after a day at work unless you had an ulterior motive. Last I heard you were complaining about not having enough time to help me. Now you've started up a class of your own? I smell a rat.'

'Okay. So, she's cute and I asked her out but she said no, so I figured if she brought Chilli Girl into puppy school, I'd get a second chance.'

'You *must* be interested. I didn't think you were hanging around here long enough to get involved with anyone?'

'A coffee or a drink is not getting involved. I don't intend marrying the girl, Mum. Sheesh.'

'Okay, who is she?'

'She's a new station hand out at Braden's place.'

Mum screwed up her face. 'She's got a golden retriever out there? That's not a working dog.'

'Yeah, I thought that too, but I think Chilli is more of a companion to her than a working dog.'

'She sounds interesting. I must meet her and invite her to the garden party.'

'No, Mum. For goodness' sake.' Ben held his temper, all the more determined to move out of his childhood home as soon as he could. He felt about fifteen.

'No, everyone's coming and I can invite who I want to. Which reminds me. Your father is going to bowls that weekend so can I depend on you for a hand?'

'Of course, you can, Mother dear. You know I won't let you down.'

'Good. Thank you.'

Ben knew why Dad wasn't staying home. His father would rather spend his weekend watching the footie or playing bowls, and not serving champagne at a garden party.

'And the same goes for you. Don't you let me down. If you do happen to meet Amelia. You just take care of what you say.'

'I'll just say one thing. It would be so nice if she turned out to be "the one" and you settle here.'

'Mum.' Ben's voice held a warning note but as usual, his mother didn't take heed.

'No, let me have my say. For the life of me, I don't know why you're hellbent on moving away. There's nothing wrong with Augathella.'

'No, there's nothing wrong with Augathella, but I'm a big boy now and I can make my own choices in life.'

The sound that came from his mother's mouth as she turned and strode down to the kitchen was extremely rude.

'Mum!'

'Not now, Ben, I'm busy. I have to go and prune the...' The back door slammed before she finished her sentence and Ben shook his head. How the heck had he managed to say so little and get Mum on his case? She did it every time; she always managed to prise every little detail out of him without him twigging to it. He'd never been able to hide anything from her, ever since he was a little tacker. The sooner he moved away, the quicker he could have some peace and quiet in his life.

He pushed away the thought that he hadn't been very content when he was living away either.

Ben went in search of a clean pair of jeans in his chest of drawers. One advantage of living at home. He didn't have to worry about washing and ironing.

The back door opened as he reached for his jeans, and his mother's voice called down the hall.

'I forgot to tell you I heard something today I thought you might be interested in.'

'What's that, Mum?'

'I had coffee with Ruth Malone.'

'Who?'

'You know, Fallon's mum.'

'Oh yeah, I know who she is. I've seen her around with Fallon. Fallon hasn't had the baby, has she?'

'No of course not, she's still got around three months to go.'

Ben zipped up his denim jeans and shrugged as he stepped into the hall. His mother was standing there with her arms folded.

'What did you hear?'

'Do you know old George Malone?'

'Yep, I remember him. The grumpy old fellow who used to live in the last house in the street on the edge of town. Where I used to go to cricket training.'

'That's the one. He's Fallon's uncle, or great uncle. Well, he went into aged care a few months ago. Fallon lived there when she first came to town. Now that she and Jon are living out at the back of Kilcoy Station, Ruth and her hubby have come to town to be close by when the baby's born, and they've all been cleaning out George's house.'

'Is there a point to this?' Ben looked pointedly at the clock at the end of the hall.

'Yes, there is. Don't be rude.'

'And the point is? Hurry up, Mum. I want to be down there by five.'

'You've got plenty of time. Just listen to me. Anyway, Ruth and Fallon have talked to George and he wants to sell the place.'

Ben stilled. 'The Malone place? It's got a bit of land with it, hasn't it?'

'Yes, I think it's got about ten acres,' his mother said. She looked innocent and he stared at her.

'So, you thought I might be interested, Mum?'

'Well, even if you insist on going away *again*, it wouldn't be bad to have a base here for when you do come home.' She grinned. 'You wouldn't have to live with your old mum and dad, and have me putting your clothes out and watching your every move.' Her lips twitched again, and he knew she had reeled him in, hook, line and sinker.

'You know I don't mind living here, Mum.'

'I know, my sweet, but you're thirty-two years old and you *shouldn't* be living with your parents.'

'Are you saying you don't want me here? I'll pack up tonight.'

'Temper, temper. You are so like your father. Of course, I'm not saying that. If you had your own place here, with your good job and all your friends here, plus you and Kent are making a real go of this singing, it would be easier for you. I just thought it might be something for you to think about.'

Ben pulled a face. 'As much as I hate saying it, Mum, okay, you've got me interested. Who should I see? Fallon, or her mum and dad?'

'I'm not sure. It wouldn't hurt to call around there one afternoon.' Her expression reminded him of Barney, Mum's spoiled cat when he beat Ben to the chair near the fire in the living room.

'I might call around tonight after puppy school.'

His mother's grin widened and her eyes were bright. 'You *are* keen, are you? I knew it would be perfect for you.'

'No. I'm just interested in seeing what's going.'

'Excellent. Now, hurry up, Ben, or you'll be late.'

'What time is it?'

'Five to five.'

'Oh shit.' This time, Ben did roll his eyes as he raced back to the Star Wars poster-covered bedroom he'd grown up in. Rummaging through his wardrobe he searched for his Guns and Roses T-shirt. He didn't want to look too formal; he probably looked a bit officious in his work clothes carrying his clipboard the other day.

He wanted to look more like himself, although Amelia had been at the concert the other night so she had seen him in his black gear and his Akubra when he was up there playing with Kent.

Maybe Craig Wilson should have had him as a raffle prize too. Ben pulled himself up short as he wrangled the T-shirt over his head.

Jeez, get over yourself, mate.

Although he did have a suspicion that the raffle prize of a date with Kent had been rigged, set up by Craig especially to get Kent and Sophie together.

It had worked. He was mighty pleased about that; Kent was happy, but the last thing Ben wanted to do was settle down. He had a lot of Queensland to see before he set up a home although the Malone house being for sale was very tempting.

He grabbed his keys and wallet and then changed his mind and rushed into the kitchen, taking the van keys off the hook near the back door.

'Mum,' he yelled out the back door. 'I'm taking your van. All the gear's in it.'

Ben was thoughtful as he hurried out to his mother's van. He knew the Malone property well; he used to go down there when he was a kid and play cricket at the back of George Malone's house. There was a crowd of boys there, enough for two teams most summer afternoons. The land was dead flat and the lawn had made a great cricket pitch; there'd been lots of fours hit across that rolling lawn on those afternoons. Old George even had a roller to roll the pitch for the boys back in those days. He'd been the president of the senior and junior cricket clubs for about twenty-five years. His name took up most of the board in the sports club.

It was a damn good property and there weren't many like it that would come on the market in Augathella. A suburban street with a solid house, but best of all were the ten acres at the back.

He had to go to Charleville for a meeting on Monday, so he'd call in and see the bank when he was there. Just an enquiry, though. Nothing more.

Even though there'd be no trouble getting a loan, he had to think if it really was a wise move to put his savings into real estate in Augathella. He'd managed to whack a fair bit of money away over the last few years. It all came down to how much it was going to sell for.

Plus, now that he was living at home again and had a local government ute, his entire pay packet stayed in the bank every fortnight. A couple of beers on a Friday night with the blokes down at the pub, and the occasional hamburger on the weekend at the footie were his only expenses. He'd tried to give Mum some board money, but she waved him off.

He and Kent had also been surprised that the local clubs were happy to pay for them to perform, and the bookings had been filling up as the word got around. Next weekend they were up at the pub at Tambo where the crowds would be gathering for the famous chicken races.

Ben was thoughtful as he pulled up at the showground. Actually, living back at Augathella was turning out better than he'd expected.

Chapter 9

As Callie turned into a street at the back of the small town, a red vintage ute drove across the intersection in front of them.

'Oh, good stuff! Fallon's in town,' Callie said. 'She must be visiting Ruth. I'm so pleased you're going to meet her. Both of them, actually. Fallon's an interesting person, I think you'll get on like a house on fire. You've met Jon, haven't you?'

'Yes, I had a meeting with Jon and Braden this morning, and Jon showed me around. I think I'm going to enjoy working at the station.' Amelia watched with interest as the old red ute pulled up in the driveway of the house.

Callie parked on the street outside the small weatherboard house. The front garden was neat and tidy, and the house looked to be in pretty good condition. Lush green paddocks behind the house caught her attention; a huge expense of land disappeared down behind the house and was dotted with a few fat and shiny steers. In the distance, she could see the glint of the river.

'You don't know how much land there is here, do you?' she asked as she opened the door, keen to see the house.

'Ruth and Fallon will be able to tell you. Come on in and you can meet them.'

Amelia reached down for Chilli's lead, and Callie lifted the three leads for the boys' dogs from the console before she climbed out of the driver's side. Amelia went around to open the door on Chilli's side just as the door of the red ute opened.

A tall, very attractive, very pregnant woman climbed carefully out of the ute and Amelia's eyes widened; Fallon was a lot bigger than she'd expected to see. Not that she knew much about pregnancy, but her stomach was *huge*. The boys came running out behind her.

'Wow, this is a welcoming committee,' Fallon said as she walked across to them. 'Hi, you must be Amelia. Jon told me all about you. Welcome to Augathella, or probably more to the point, welcome to Kilcoy Station.'

'Thank you, it's good to be here. I enjoyed talking to Jon this morning. And I like Augathella too.'

'Holy hell, Fallon. You like look like you're just about ready to pop this bub out,' Callie put her hand on Fallon's stomach, keeping one eye on the boys as they secured the leads to the dogs' collars.

'Ages to go yet. Besides, we're not ready for him yet. We've still got a lot of painting and tiling to do.'

'Him?' Callie said.

'Yep, not a secret. Not twins either. Can't see the point in keeping it quiet.'

'The boys will be excited. And you're well?' Callie asked.

'Fit as a fiddle.' Fallon laughed. 'But a fat fiddle.'

They all walked across the footpath to the front gate. Rory, Nigel, and Petie were holding the dogs' leads and Chilli barked as if to say "wait for me" as they ran ahead through the gate. Amelia knew her eyes were wide as she looked around. The house had such a welcoming and homely feel to it.

'Amelia wants to know a little bit about your uncle's place,' Callie said.

'Uncle George's place?' Fallon rolled her eyes. 'We've been cleaning it out for ages. I'm just so glad Mum and Dad turned up to help. Dad's been helping Jon sort out the sheds. We've taken so much to the op shop in town, I swear Val locks the door when she sees us coming!'

'Did your uncle pass away recently?' Amelia asked.

'No, he's in the aged care facility up the road. He actually wanted me to move into the old place. Said he'd leave it to me.'

'And you're not moving in?' Amelia looked around the garden.

'No. I find being in town claustrophobic. We're happy out on the land. But I didn't say no to Uncle George's fabulous ute. I told him to sell the place and make some money while he's still alive. But he said he's got no need for it. Mum and Dad don't want to move out here. They're going back to Brisbane in a little while, so we talked to George and he's agreed to sell the place.' She looked curiously at Amelia. 'Are you really interested? It'll go for a song. It's pretty hard to sell places out here now. Everyone's moving away, even if it's only to Charleville.'

'I am looking to settle somewhere,' Amelia said, not wanting to sound too keen. 'I'm not quite sure where yet, but Augathella is looking good so far. I've had a really good impression of the town and what's on. It's such a friendly place. The local cattle industry seems to be booming so there'll always be lots of work, but I'm looking for a place of my own. A house that's got enough land that I can run a few cattle of my own and bring my horse down from the Gulf.'

'The Gulf? Were you working up there?' Fallon asked.

'Yeah, sort of. My Mum and Dad own Granite Springs.'

'I know it. I did some mustering not far from there a couple of years back. It's one of the biggest spreads up there.' The look Fallon was giving her now was full of interest.

'Do you work on the land too?' Amelia asked, just as interested in Fallon's background.

'I'm a helicopter pilot,' Fallon replied. 'I did aerial mustering up in the Territory and North Queensland for a few years before I moved down here late last year.' Fallon patted her stomach. 'Long story short. I fell in love with the boss, and we've moved in together. But there won't be any helicopter flying at the moment, and probably not for a while after the bub.'

'Do you miss it?' Amelia asked.

'I do but not as much as I expected. I'm keeping busy. Jon and I are doing up the old house we're living in at the back of Kilcoy Station.'

'It's the house that Braden and Sophie grew up in,' Callie said.

'Yeah, the original homestead. We're doing the work in exchange for Braden letting us stay there.'

Fallon opened the front gate, Callie and Amelia behind her and the boys came running over.

'Callie, Callie. Guess what Ruth made for us? Some pink lamingtons and we're allowed to have lemonade too, in little cups called tumblers.' Petie's words tumbled over each other. 'If you say yes, we can, she said.'

Amelia looked up at the older woman who walked out of the house with a sheepish smile on her face.

'I hope that was alright, Callie.'

'Of course, it is. It doesn't hurt the boys to have a treat occasionally. I won't tell you they had Tim Tams and potato chips for dinner the other night amid all the excitement.'

Ruth laughed. 'The night you get engaged is a pretty special night.'

Callie rolled her eyes. 'Don't tell me the news has got to town already?'

Ruth's smile was wide. 'Sweetie, you'll get used to a small country town, quick smart. Nothing stays private here for very long.' She turned to Amelia who was hanging back as they all chatted. 'Hello, and welcome, don't be shy,' she said. 'You must be Amelia. I heard you were coming in with Callie. Welcome to Augathella, although I can't really say that because I'm not a true local myself, although a semi-local, I suppose. I used to come out and visit George when I was a young girl.'

Fallon glanced over at her mum. 'Amelia might be interested in having a look at the place. Have you listed it with the real estate agent yet?'

'No,' Ruth said. 'I haven't got around to it yet, but Amelia, if you're serious, you're more than welcome to have a look around.'

'How much land is there?' Amelia asked.

'Ah, I think there's around ten acres from the back of the house to the boundary near the river, but I can find out exactly if you want.'

Amelia's eyes grew wide. 'Ten acres? Wow, that sounds great.'

'Anyway, you can have a look around the place and have a think about it. I think most people in town think we're waiting for poor George to pass on before we sell it. It certainly hasn't been advertised yet and I don't know that it's going to sell very quickly. But one thing I'd hate is to see someone come out from the city and play at being a country farmer.'

Amelia saw the hurt look on Callie's face, and Ruth must have noticed too.

'Ah Callie, I don't mean you, I know how much you love it out here.'

'I know that, Ruth.'

Ruth held the small iron gate open as the girls walked through. Callie and Fallon were chatting ahead of her, and Amelia smiled her thanks as she walked through with Chilli Girl. The minute she stepped onto the path edged by two narrow gardens a shiver ran down her back. Not an unpleasant shiver, at all. She looked around at the neatly mown and fenced yard, the edges of the path trimmed and the gardens free of weeds. It appealed to her so much, she wasn't game to look at the house in case she was disappointed.

'What do you think, Chilli Girl? It's a lovely big garden, isn't it? How good would it be to play ball here?'

Chilli barked and Amelia smiled at her. 'Yes, girl, I think it would be fun too.'

Typical Amelia, she could just hear her father saying. *No thought, no logic, just go with the flow of what you want at the time. Don't you, girlie?*

The "girlie" was always said in the same disparaging tone.

Maybe she was adopted?

Maybe Mum had had an affair with a station hand, and that cranky old man wasn't even her father.

'Amelia?'

'Oh sorry, Ruth. I was miles away.'

'I asked if would you like a cup of tea or coffee? Callie said you've got an hour or so before you have to be at the showground.'

'Yes, please. Coffee would be great.'

'Come on in. It's a bit warmer in the kitchen. You must find it cold here after the Gulf.'

'The past few mornings have been cool. Chilli climbed up in the van with me the other morning before we moved out to the station, poor baby.' Amelia swallowed as she followed Ruth over to the back door. Callie and Fallon were near the fence with the three boys and the pups.

'There's a hen sitting on eggs over there. Petie's been keeping guard since he came here from kindy.'

'Oh. Will Chilli be all right out here? I'd better stay out with her.'

'It's fine. Look, Petie and the boys have a handle on the situation.'

Amelia smiled as she looked over there. True enough the three boys had formed a wall at the edge of the garden.

'Won't the ground be too cold now that the cold weather's coming?'

Ruth chuckled. 'My husband's been putting a gas heater out there each night. It's the most spoiled chook in Augathella. They're not far off hatching and then we can bring them inside.'

'I like that. How thoughtful of him.'

Ruth laughed again. 'We're not country people by a long shot, but Fallon's been teaching us. Come in, come in. Your dog will be fine.'

Amelia took a deep breath and followed Ruth. The screen door was an old-fashioned one. A rectangle of gauze was tacked onto a green-painted timber frame. The door squeaked as it swung shut behind them.

A cosy kitchen filled with the smell of fresh baking, and the accompanying warmth from a combustion stove greeted them. Trays of biscuits lined the benches as well as the pink lamingtons that the boys had mentioned. Pretty red and white checked curtains framed the window that overlooked the back garden and out over the acres that stretched as far as she could see. Amelia's eyes widened and warmth filled her as she imagined living here. She shook herself out of her daydream when she realised Ruth was watching her with a smile on her face.

'You've been busy, Ruth,' Amelia said. 'It smells wonderful.'

'I'm helping out with the cooking for the garden party that's coming up. A fundraiser for the RFDS. Most of this lot will go in the deep freeze.'

'That's good of you. They'll sell on aroma alone.' Amelia pulled a face. 'Very different to our place. Mum's garden parties are catered for by fly-in caterers from Darwin.'

The more Amelia heard about this town, the more she liked it, and the more she thought maybe she could settle here. 'May I look through the rest of the house?' she asked timidly. 'Would that be okay?'

'Of course, sweetie. Feel free to have a wander through and poke in all the rooms. We're just caretaking for a while, so have a good look. Most of the stuff in the rooms is George's, and we have to decide whether to keep or give it away. Mind you, it looks a lot better now than it did three months ago. Take your time, I'll put the jug on.'

As Amelia stepped into the wide hallway, she heard the back door open and Ruth tell the others she was looking around the house.

The voices and the smell of home baking faded as she stepped through the house. The carpet was old and faded but clean. The bathroom had a pink bathtub and old-fashioned vanity basin, but she loved it. Three bedrooms, all with large proportions came off the hallway and at the front, a glassed-in porch looked out over the quiet street, and then across to more paddocks. The house reminded her of Gran's house in Normanton, where no one ever came to the front door. Everyone was welcomed through the kitchen.

She turned around and went back to the kitchen where the three women were sitting around the red Laminex kitchen table.

'Have a seat, Amelia. Your coffee's there, and there's milk and sugar in the pink jugs.' Ruth pointed to the mug in front of the empty chair.

'Oh, how lovely. My gran had that same jug with the cow face. Now I really feel like I'm at home.'

Fallon and Ruth shared a hopeful look and Amelia smiled.

'I'd really love to come back and have a good look. Perhaps you could let me know when I do how much you would be asking?'

Chapter 10

Callie looked at her phone.

'Time we went to the showground. Jenny will be waiting for us.'

'Thanks so much for the coffee and lamingtons, Ruth,' Amelia said. 'It was so good to see the house. My dad always tells me that I rush into things, but I'll come into town when I have my first day off. Does that suit your schedule or are you in a rush to sell?'

'Sweetie, this is Augathella,' Ruth said with a wide smile. 'An old place might take quite a while to sell, although the land might be of interest to some. I'd hate to see the old house knocked down for the land.'

'Oh no. Do you think that could happen?' Amelia decided to get back as fast as she could. Maybe even after she'd knocked off one afternoon? It all depended on what Jon had lined up for her, and whether she'd be out on the property in a swag at night.

'Well, like I said, I'm interested, but I guess if you have an offer before I get the chance to have a better look and get my finances organised, you just have to take the first offer. I'd hate you to wait around and then I decided it wasn't for me, so just take note that I'm interested but if someone else is, just let me know maybe.'

Amelia followed Callie outside and Callie called the boys. They'd gone back outside with the dogs. 'Come on, kids, it's time to go to puppy school and see Jenny.'

Amelia followed slowly. The house was sweet and she loved the land around it. It just felt right; it was as though the house had been waiting for her to come to Augathella. She'd stayed in a few places on her way south but none had welcomed her as much as this little town.

With ten acres she could run a few cattle and have a chook pen. She could get her horse from home and there was enough work around at the surrounding properties that she could still get work after her contract at Kilcoy Station was completed. Maybe she'd stay there; Braden and Callie seemed to like her so far, but she guessed it would depend on whether Braden and Jon were happy with her work. She had no doubt she could prove herself.

Callie must have read her thoughts. 'It would be so good to have you in town, Amelia.'

'I think it would be good to be here.'

Callie looked at her curiously, probably wondering why someone of her age was looking to resettle by herself, but she didn't ask.

'Heaps of us here you can be friends with, so you won't be lonely if you buy the property.'

'I don't want to rush in, but between you and me, I'm really keen.' Amelia crouched down as Chilli came running over to her. 'Have you been a good girl? Are you going to be a good girl at puppy school?' She turned to Callie who was hurrying the boys up. 'Do you know who runs the puppy school Callie?' she asked.

'Yes, it's Mrs Riley. She's lovely.'

'Riley?' Amelia frowned. 'Is she related to Ben?'

'I'm pretty sure she's his mum. I'm still new enough in town to be learning who's related to who. I met her in town once. She happened to be putting the poster up on the community noticeboard and I asked about it. I'm glad you told me it was tonight because I thought it was on Saturday afternoons.' She lowered her voice as the boys climbed into the four-wheel drive. 'Between you and me, I'll be really interested to see how the boys go. The pups have got a bit out of hand. It'll be good for the boys to learn some structure. I'm not much good. I've never had a dog. And Braden's been too busy to teach them.'

'This should be good for them. I really don't know why *we* have to be here though. Chilli has good habits and is obedient, but Mr High and Mighty Riley decreed we had to come. I hope his mum is nicer than he is.'

'She is. She's a lovely lady, friends with Ruth, she said. I met her again at Fallon and Jon's engagement drink at the pub. I'm pretty sure she is his mum, but I could be wrong. They are related though, I think. He wasn't there that night. He and Kent were singing down in Charleville.'

'Engaged? I thought they were married?'

'They are. They slipped away and got married quietly a couple of months ago. Just the two of them, with her parents as witnesses. Fallon's not one for fuss and bother.'

'That's a shame. If I ever get married, I want the full works. The big white wedding in a church.' She grinned but sadness tugged at her. 'I can't see my father giving me away. He already has.'

'What do you mean?'

'Me and Dad? That's a long story. One for over a drink one night. Actually, he'd probably be really pleased to give me away to someone. To get me out of his hair once and for all.'

'We'll have that drinks' night. It's probably time to organise another girls' night out, and you can meet some of the others. You know, I've socialised more in Augathella than I ever did in Brisbane.' Callie held the dogs' leads as the boys climbed into the four-wheel drive. 'I've been telling my best friend in Brissie about this town, and she's going to bring her kids out for a visit. She's also going to be the matron of honour at the wedding. Mind you, I think it's more to do with checking out Braden! So, don't worry, there's plenty for you to do here. You'll never be bored.'

'I like my own company, and now I've got Chilli, I've got someone to talk to. I'd be quite happy living in old George's house on the edge of town. I could be a happy spinster looking after some chooks, and cows.'

'Don't speak too soon, sweetie. That was my philosophy up till six months ago when my almost fiancé at the time did the dirty on me. Look at me now! Engaged and about to become a step mum to three fabulous little boys.'

'When's the wedding?'

Callie smiled. 'That's the next thing we have to decide. Life is so busy!' She opened the back of the Landcruiser station wagon and lifted the three puppies in. 'Put Chilli in the front with us. We only have a short way to go.'

Amelia put her arms beneath Chilli and lifted her up. 'Oh my God, girl, I think I need to put you on a diet. You're growing way too fast.' Amelia climbed in after her and looped her fingers through Chilli's collar. 'So where are we going? I mean where is it held? Inside or outside?'

'Well, it used to be at the showground but now that you mention it, I'm not sure whether it's there or at the park. I'll give Ben a call. His number's in my phone.'

Callie started the car and put the phone on speaker as she pulled out onto the road and turned the corner towards the main street.

'Ben Riley.'

Amelia turned away as *his* voice came over the speaker.

'Hey Ben, how's it going? It's Callie Young here. We're on our way to puppy school with your mum and I'm not sure where it's being held. At the showground or the park?'

Amelia's heart took a leap and she tried not to listen as Ben's voice came over the car audio. 'Hey, Callie. It's at the showground. I'm looking forward to seeing the boys there.'

Amelia widened her eyes and her fingers tightened automatically on Chilli's collar. *He* was going to be there too.

'Okay, see you there in five. We're not far away.'

'See ya.'

Amelia turned to Callie. 'Did you know Ben was going to be there tonight too?'

Callie turned a wide-eyed innocent look in her direction. 'I think Ben helps out sometimes.'

'So this is a bit of a setup, is it?' Amelia folded her arms. 'I don't even know why he insisted that I bring Chilli in.'

'A setup? No, not at all. Chilli bit Ben, so he's right saying she needs some obedience lessons.' Callie followed the main street along and followed the sign to the showground.

'She didn't bite him. She just tore his trousers a little bit.'

Callie raised her eyebrows, but she didn't comment.

Amelia pulled out her bag and took out a comb, loosened the scrunchie around her ponytail and brushed her hair back and re-tied it. She glanced over at Callie, but she was innocently watching the road ahead.

Surreptitiously, Amelia reached into her bag and twisted the lid off a small pot of lip gloss and put a little bit on her finger and rubbed it on her lips. Pinching her cheeks until she knew her fair skin would have some colour she sat back and smoothed her T-shirt down over her jeans. If she had to see Mr Riley, she'd look tidy.

***

Ben drove towards the showground resisting the temptation of turning down Jane Street for a quick look at George Malone's place. He didn't have time. He wanted to be set up before his class arrived.

He cursed under his breath as he parked behind Braden's Landcruiser on Roselyn Road. They'd got there before him. He jumped out and quickly walked around and opened the back of the van and pulled out the six plastic chairs and the dog mats.

Callie and the boys were in the middle of the show ring with Amelia and Chilli Girl. The boys' yells were punctuated by Chilli's deep woof as they chased three small but energetic dogs around.

Once he had the chairs and mats set up, he walked around to the back of the wagon and pulled out a bag of pigs' ears and some liver treats.

Amelia and the boys and the dogs stayed out in the middle of the field.

Callie spotted him setting up and walked over, 'Hi, Ben. Your mum's not here yet?' She looked across at the van.

'Mum's not coming tonight. I decided to do an extra class so we could keep you all together.'

'Thanks for that. The boys are really excited. Will I get them over now?'

'Yep, if we start now, we'll have a good hour before dark.'

Ben grinned as Callie put her hand to her mouth and let out a sharp whistle. She gestured to the group in the middle and the boys took off towards them, followed closely by the three dogs, and more slowly by Amelia who had her hand on Chilli's collar.

'I've got some things to do at school. Are you okay if I leave you with the boys and Amelia and the four dogs, or would you rather I hung around?'

'No, that's fine, you do whatever you have to do.'

'About an hour you said?'

'Yes, we'll just do the basics tonight and let the dogs settle in. Have the boys' dogs learned any skills yet?'

Callie shook her head. 'They've got some pretty bad habits. The boys spoil them rotten. Braden's always roaring at them and telling them to make them sit down and stay and do things like that, but the boys and the pups all do what they want. He's taking it slowly with them—the boys I mean—but it's going to come to a head soon. He found Cottie asleep with Petie in his bed the other morning.'

'Okay, I'll stress to the boys that the pups need a routine.'

'You've got your work cut out, I think.'

'Not a problem. Been there, done that. I know what to do. It'll probably take the six sessions to see a difference, but if you can get the boys practising at home it'll reinforce it.'

'With both the dogs and the boys.' Callie laughed. 'Braden's finally realising that he doesn't have to go so soft on them. It's not doing them any favours; they're getting out of line.'

'It's been a hard time for all of you,' Ben said, glancing across as Amelia stood back waiting for them to finish talking. Her dark hair was pulled back in a high ponytail and her fair cheeks had that rosy glow. She really was a pretty woman.

Callie saw him looking at Amelia and a smile played around her lips.

'And you're right with Amelia and Chilli too?'

'Yeah, all good. I guess Amelia wasn't real keen on coming. Has Chilli behaved with the other dogs?'

'She loves them, and the boys. She hasn't been aggressive at all, although she did tear your trousers the other day.'

'Yeah. She wasn't happy to see me. I'll be watching her.'

The dog under discussion sat sedately beside her mistress.

'As far as I can see, she's placid and she seems to do what she's told. I've got no idea why she bit you that day.'

'I think she thought I was threatening Amelia. I did come up very suddenly from behind the building and it's not a bad thing that a dog will protect their mistress like that.'

'So, there's no need for Chilli to be here at puppy school?' This time Callie grinned and they shared a look.

'There is a need,' Ben replied. 'We'll wait and see how she goes.'

'Okay, I'll see you in an hour or so.'

Callie crouched down next to the boys and Amelia continued to stand back. Ben waited as Callie gave the boys instructions.

'Now, you all listen carefully to Ben and do what he says. I'll be back soon, okay?'

They all nodded and Ben waited until Callie was in the car before he turned to greet them. For some reason he felt nervous; strange because it hadn't been that long since he'd run a class.

Amelia was watching him with a closed expression.

'Welcome boys, and hello, Amelia.'

She nodded without speaking.

'Now I'd like you all to introduce me to your dogs and I'll show you the right way to greet a dog you haven't met before.'

Ben turned over his right hand and held it out as Rory walked over with a reddish-brown dog. Ben glanced across at the other two; it looked like they were all from the same litter.

He crouched down as the small dog hesitantly sniffed at the back of his hand. 'What's his name, Rory?'

'His name is Bumper. I called him that because when I lay down on the ground with him when he was a little pup, he liked to bump my head.'

'An excellent name,' he said. Glancing up, Ben finally caught the glimmer of a smile from Amelia.

Nigel ran over, his dog nipping at his heels.

A bad habit, Ben thought.

'This is Tweedle. He's my dog,' Nigel said puffing his chest out as the dog licked Ben's hand and then turned to roll over with Bumper. 'Tweedle Dee is his full name.'

'From the story?' Ben asked.

'No.' Nigel screwed his face up. 'It's from a nursery rhyme that Aunty Sophie made up for us.'

This time Ben and Amelia's eyes connected and her smile was wide. She came over to Nigel and put her hand on his shoulder. 'There's a Tweedle Dee and Tweedle Dum in one of my favourite stories about a girl called Alice.'

'I don't like girl stories,' Nigel said with a pout. 'Actually, I don't like girls very much. They're a bit silly. They giggle and Callie gets cross at them in the playground.'

'You might change your mind when you get a bit older, mate.' Ben was pleased to see that Amelia looked a bit more relaxed, but she was still hanging tightly onto Chilli.

Nigel shrugged and Ben turned to little Petie 'Now Petie's turn. Introduce me to your pup.'

'This is my Cottie and she's the bestest behaved dog in our family.' Petie leaned over and cupped his hand over Ben's ear, his breath warm on his cheek. 'Dad said that's because I look after her the bestest, but don't tell Nigel and Rory that.'

Ben lowered his voice. 'I won't tell.'

'Now boys, while I meet Amelia's dog, I'd like you to sit on the chairs and get your pups on the mat in front of your feet. If they won't stay there, you can get one treat each out of the bag and give it to them to get them to sit quietly. Can you do that?'

The three boys nodded and did as they were asked, and Ben finally turned to Amelia. 'Hello, Amelia, I'm pleased to see you here.'

Her chin lifted a fraction, but his gaze honed in on her pink lips, shiny with gloss. For a moment his thoughts left him, and he shook his head to try to remember what he'd been going to say.

Finally, his head cleared. 'May I talk to Chilli?'

She nodded. 'You may.'

He moved across to stand in front of the dog who stood quietly next to her mistress. Holding his handout, he said quietly. 'Hello, Chilli Girl.'

The golden Labrador looked at him with something akin to adoration in her eyes and Ben grinned.

'That's a much nicer welcome, Chilli.' He lifted his head and caught a strange look on Amelia's face as he met her eyes. 'Come on over and sit down, and see if Chilli will sit in front of you,' he said.

Her eyebrows rose. 'Chilli will do whatever I tell her to. There is no need for us to be here.'

Ben shook his head. 'I beg to differ. Even though she seems happy to see me tonight, there was still her reaction the other day. We have to understand what caused that.'

Amelia's lips pursed and she moved across to one of the empty chairs. She pointed to the mat, and didn't even speak. The look she flashed him as Chilli sat quietly at her feet was triumphant.

Ben surveyed his class with a smile. Three little boys and one pretty woman sat on the chairs with four well behaved dogs sitting at their feet. Granted, Tweedle and Bumper had needed a treat to sit down, but Petie's Cottie, and Chilli, had obeyed the simple instruction.

Ben settled into the class and began to enjoy himself, forgetting for a while that it was Amelia sitting there. Over the hour, she seemed to relax and he was pleased to hear her laugh at one point. The only downside was Nigel's reluctance to follow instructions.

A couple of times Ben stood close to Amelia as he taught her some quick tricks to get Chilli's attention, and a waft of something floral surrounded him.

Too soon the sound of a vehicle caught his attention, and he looked up as a car door slammed. Callie was walking across to them.

Petie let go of Cottie's lead and ran across to meet her. Ben smiled as he wrapped his arms around Callie's jean-clad legs. 'Oh, Callie, we've had the bestest time, and Cottie was the bestest dog.'

'He was not.' Nigel's face reddened with anger as he almost yelled. 'You're just a baby, Petie. What would you know about dogs!'

Ben went to intervene but held back when Amelia caught his eye and shook her head slightly. Callie walked over to Nigel and put her hand on his shoulder. 'That wasn't very nice, Nigel. I want you to say sorry to Petie.'

Nigel glared up at her. 'No.'

'Nigel, you are—'

'You're not my mother and you can't tell me what to do.'

Ben and Amelia looked at each other, and Ben felt sorry for Callie and more than a bit helpless. He didn't know whether to intervene or leave it to Callie to handle the situation. He decided to stay quiet and not give in to Nigel's demand for attention.

Callie's teacher training came to the fore as she defused the situation and took the attention off Nigel. 'Rory, Petie, say thank you to Ben and then take Bumper and Cottie and get in the car and wait for us please.' She ignored Nigel who stared after his brothers as they thanked Ben and ran off to the car. When the boys were in the car, Ben was surprised when Amelia turned to him and held her hand out.

'Thank you, Ben. I've learned a lot tonight.'

He took her hand and shook it gently, maybe holding on for longer than necessary. Finally, he let go and she dropped her gaze.

'Same time next week suit?' he asked.

'Um, I'm not sure. I'll be at work by then, and I could be out on the property but we'll sort something.' With a quick smile, she tugged on Chilli's lead and they headed off to the car.

Callie put her hand on Nigel's shoulder. 'Right, young man, your turn.'

'My turn to what?' came the sullen reply.

'To say what we're waiting for.'

'What?'

'You know, Nigel. Manners please.'

Nigel lifted his chin and the look he shot Callie was full of venom. 'Okay. I'll say it. Petie is a little turd and I hate you.'

Ben couldn't help himself. 'Nigel! I'm very disappointed in you.'

Callie shook her head. 'Thanks, Ben, we'll get going now. I'll give you a call about next week.' Her eyes were awash with tears and Ben's heart broke for her. Nigel was still carrying a lot of grief inside, the poor little bloke, and Ben hoped that the situation wouldn't impact on Braden and Callie's relationship.

He put his hand out to Callie, and she dropped her gaze as she took it briefly before she let go and took hold of Nigel's shoulder.

'You take care, Callie.'

'I will, Ben. Now, to the car, Nigel.'

To Ben's relief, the little boy bent down and picked up Tweedle and took off towards the car.

After they had driven off, he packed up the chairs and mats and carried them to the car.

He wondered how they could help Nigel, and then his thoughts turned to Amelia. She had responded to him tonight and that had made him all the more determined to ask her out. He wondered whether she was just being polite, although they had seemed to connect a few times.

Hopefully, he'd get a yes this time.

Chapter 11

'Mummy. Nigel pinched me.'

Amelia froze as Petie's plaintive little cry filled the car.

Mummy? That was guaranteed to stir Nigel up even more.

'*She's* not our mother. Our mother's dead. We don't need a new mother. We've got Aunty Sophie. I want you to go away.'

Petie started to cry and Amelia glanced at Callie. Her eyes were full of tears and her hands were white as she gripped the steering wheel. The journey up until now had been quiet and Amelia judged they were past halfway back to the station.

Assistance came from an unexpected quarter. 'Nigel, shut up. You're being mean.' Rory leaned forward from the back seat and put his hand on Callie's shoulder. 'Don't cry, Callie. Petie and I both love you lots. And if Petie wants to call you Mummy, I think that's okay too. I was even thinking about that last night, when you and Daddy get married. It's going to be good. When are you going to get married? It would be cool if it was soon. I think that would make Dad really happy.'

Amelia didn't know what to say or where to look. Callie's shoulders were shaking and tears rolled down her cheeks.

Amelia spoke quietly. 'Would you like me to drive, Callie?'

Callie shook her head and she took one hand from the steering wheel and brushed the back of her hand over her eyes. 'I'm okay, but thank you.'

Amelia half-turned in the passenger seat and looked over into the back. Nigel's face was bright red and he stared out the window chewing at his lip. Rory had his arm around little Petie who'd stopped crying.

'Who knows how to play I Spy?' she said brightly.

##

Keeping the kids focused on the I Spy game—even Nigel eventually joined in—and keeping an eye on Callie took all of Amelia's energy on the way home. Dusk had come in quickly and it was too dark to see past the headlights now. Callie was watching the road carefully and Amelia kept her eyes peeled for wildlife. The trip seemed to take forever; her heart went out to Callie; she looked so upset.

As they approached the main gate of Kilcoy Station, Callie finally spoke. Her voice was husky and full of tears. 'Amelia, could I ask you not to say anything about what's been said here? I need to think before I talk to Braden. I need to decide what to do.'

'Okay, your turn, Rory,' Amelia said brightly. The boys were making enough noise in the back to cover their conversation in the front.

'Dead tree,' Nigel yelled.

'Donga,' Petie said. For a pre-schooler, she was impressed with how well he knew his letters.

'Dark! You're both wrong. And Petie there's no dongas out here.'

Amelia turned to Callie. 'I won't say anything,' she said quietly. 'But promise me you won't do anything silly like taking off in the middle of the night.'

Callie's smile was sad. 'Are you a mind reader? I've already done that once. I've run away before. But I thought that had had a happy ending. Maybe not.'

Amelia shook her head. 'Callie, there's obviously more behind this. I'm no child psychologist, but Nigel is hurting. He's been fine since I arrived. Something's happened to bring this on, and you're his target to make him feel better.' She shook her head. 'Trust me, I know how cruel kids can be in an attempt to make themselves feel better. Please don't do anything rash. Sit down and talk to Braden tonight.'

Callie's head shake was emphatic. 'I can't make him choose. He shouldn't have to choose between me and his kids. If I go, he'll get over it. He must put his boys first.'

Amelia held back a sigh. She felt totally useless. 'Well, just promise me that if you do decide to do anything like that, you'll tell me. Promise?'

Callie nodded. 'Okay.' She took one hand off the steering wheel and reached over and squeezed Amelia's hand. 'And thank you. I'm sorry you've been brought into our troubles. You've only been here five minutes and you've been drawn into it.'

'Things will get better. There's always a solution and I'm sure you and Braden can get to the bottom of it together.'

'I'll do what needs to be done. What's best for Braden and the boys.'

Amelia stared at Callie and her voice was firm. 'Don't you leave yourself out of the equation. Your happiness is important too, Callie. And I've seen how you and Braden are together. Your love for each other shines out, and the boys will all be a part of that.'

Callie lowered her voice as the noise in the back had reduced slightly. 'I think Braden and I got engaged too soon. But thanks for caring, Amelia. It's good to have you here. As a friend.'

Amelia chuckled in an attempt to lighten the heavy atmosphere. 'I'm glad, because I feel like an imposter at the moment. I haven't done any work yet, and Braden put me on the payroll from today.'

'It's the nature of this town, the whole area, I've found. And you've been helping! It may not be cattle work, but you've already put your stamp on the place. I'm very pleased you're here. Thank you for caring.'

It was dark when they drove into the house yard towards the shed, but the back lights illuminated the path to the gate. Braden came out of the house.

Callie pulled up but left the motor running. 'You all get out here, and I'll put the car away.'

Amelia opened her door and then went to the passenger door at the back. As she lifted Petie out, Braden came across and opened the other side. She was pleased to see that Nigel was more subdued, but Braden looked at his middle son; Nigel's eyes were noticeably red.

'How did you all go? Do we have obedient dogs now?' He smiled at Amelia.

Rory scrambled out and headed around to the back to let the dogs out. 'We have to do lots of practice, Dad.' He looked at his two brothers as Braden lifted the small dogs down. 'Nigel and Petie, you go and put the dogs away and give them their tea.' He lowered his voice. 'I need to talk to Dad.'

Nigel shot him a sour look as Amelia reached for Chilli's lead and helped her down.

'Thanks for taking me in,' she called out to Callie as the car began to move towards the big shed.

Callie gave her a wave. 'No problem.'

'Come on, Chilli, we'll go and get you settled for the night.'

'To save you cooking, Amelia, would you like to join us for dinner? I've got the barbie heating up,' Braden asked.

Rory tugged at his arm. 'Dad, I have to talk to you before Callie comes back.' The other two had disappeared towards the dog pens.

'Thanks for the offer, but I'll take a rain check, Braden. A bowl of soup and some toast will do me. It's been a big day. I'll see you all tomorrow.'

'Okay, if you need anything, just yell out. Our freezers are full,' Braden said. 'And thank you. I'm sure you helped out with these three terrors.'

As Amelia walked away, she heard Braden talk to Rory. 'What's up, mate?'

'Dad, Nigel was really, really mean to Callie and she was crying. Can you fix it, please? I don't want her to go away like Mummy did.'

Amelia picked up the pace before she could hear what Braden said. As sad as she was for them, it wasn't her business.

She heard Braden tell the boys to go inside, and he ran over to the shed, his shoulders sagging, his strides long as he made his way over to the shed and Callie.

Chapter 12

Amelia poured a can of tomato soup into a bowl and put it in the microwave. While it heated, she made some toast, and when the soup was hot, she loaded a tray and headed out to the back porch of the donga. Even though it was well and truly dark, she loved sitting out there, watching the sky, and listening to the comforting sounds of the bush. She was far enough away from the main house so that she couldn't see the lights or hear any sound from it. So far, she hadn't seen anyone in the donga next to hers. There had been some activity close by during the day where three more dongas were being built. Between the building works, the kids and the dogs, there was always something happening at Kilcoy Station.

The soup was warming and her wool poncho protected her from the chill wind. The lowing and snuffling of cattle in the paddock closest to the dongas carried on the wind and made her feel at home. As she ate her thoughts turned to the events of the day.

She hoped that Braden had given Nigel a good talking to, although maybe he needed to be shown he was loved more than getting into trouble. It was a hard call, and one she knew she wouldn't be able to make. Since she'd set off from home, her future seemed so uncertain. She had no desire to settle down with a partner, and until she'd met the three little Cartwright boys and discovered that she was a natural talking to them—and enjoyed it—the thought of having kids in the foreseeable future had never once crossed her mind.

Then she had to decide what to do about that house. Logic—not that she had much of that if she listened to Dad—well, logic told her it would be a stupid thing to do. She'd arrived in this town to work with cattle, and not to go looking at houses.

But oh, how she'd loved it. And how her heart was telling her to go ahead and buy it. There was no place for logic; it was your heart you had to follow.

Her face scrunched up as Ben Riley came into her thoughts.

Now there was something her heart—well maybe not so much her heart, but parts of her that were located a tiny bit lower than her heart—were telling her to take notice of their cries.

Her sex life was pretty non-existent, and that long-neglected part of her had only flared to life because Ben Riley was such an attractive guy.

Okay, so she hadn't noticed it before. When he'd been on the stage at that Easter concert, he'd been in black in the background while Kent took the front of the stage with his singing.

And then when he'd rocked up near the donga the other day and Chilli had gone for him—although that was a harsh way to put it—all she'd seen was an officious cranky man carrying a clipboard.

The Ben Riley of tonight had set her hormones clamouring for attention. His well-muscled arms in that sexy tight T-shirt, his kindness and patience with the boys, not to mention the times she'd snagged his gaze and could have drowned in those dark brown eyes, had hit her for six, and that was not on.

She was here to work. She'd already knocked back the offer of a date, and she would continue to do so.

As if on cue, her phone rang. She jumped up and hurried inside and picked it up, but it was an unknown number.

'Hello?' she said tentatively, waiting for someone to try to sell her solar panels or life insurance.

'Hey, Amelia, it's Ben.' Her traitorous body jumped straight to attention. 'I hope you don't mind; I got your number from Braden. I had to persuade him though.'

She smiled. 'That's okay. What's up? Was Chilli too hard for you to handle tonight?'

'No, she was great. I . . .um. . . I was hoping you'd come out to dinner with me tomorrow night.' He rushed on before she could answer. 'I haven't had many weekends free lately, because Kent and I are getting a few gigs. He asked for this weekend off because he's taking Sophie away, so I wondered if I could take you to dinner. To apologise for being such a jerk when we first met.'

Her words seemed to be creating themselves and Amelia surprised herself when they left her lips almost before he'd stopped talking. 'I'd love to.'

Where did that come from?

'You would?'

'Yeah, a night out would be good before I start work next week. Where to?'

She could hear the smile in his voice.

'Well, there's the pub or the—'

'Or the pub,' she finished for him.

His chuckle gave her goosebumps. Nice ones.

'Yep, the pub, unless you want to drive to Charleville. There's a great pub there. Lots of history and great meals.'

'The local pub will be fine. I don't want to go too far yet. I'm still learning the local district.'

'Trust me, that won't take too long. Great. I'll pick you up at five tomorrow.'

'There's no need to come out of town. I can drive in.'

'No. If I have a date, I insist on being a gentleman.'

Her common sense came to the fore.

About time.

'It's not a date, Ben. It's an apology.'

He laughed again and those damn goosebumps danced up and down her spine. 'Okay, I'll pick you up for my apology. See you tomorrow night.'

'Okay, I'll call you if something comes up.'

'See you tomorrow, Amelia.'

The call disconnected before she could say another word, but there was a smile on her face.

Whoever would have thought the shire inspector who'd pushed her buttons a few days ago was now pushing them in a very different way?

Amelia picked up her plates and spoon and headed inside. The wind had picked up and she was getting cold. As she rinsed her plates, her phone rang again, and she smiled.

What did he want now?

'Hello again,' she answered and then straightened as a female voice replied.

'Amelia, it's Callie. I hope I didn't wake you?'

'Heck no, I've just had dinner. Been sitting out the back enjoying the landscape. Everything okay?'

'Yes, all good, but I have a huge favour to ask. If you can't or don't want to, just say no, and we'll change our plans.'

'What do you need?'

'We've had a big heart-to-heart here, and we're still worried about Nigel. He's got himself in a real state. Braden rang the doctor, but he's away, and the new doctor answered. He wants us to come in first thing in the morning. I called Sophie but she and Kent are going away for the weekend. We just need someone to watch the other two boys. I know it's not your role here—'

'Stop right now. Of course, I will. I'm free all day. And forget about roles, it's what friends do. And I love those boys already. We'll have a great time.'

Callie's voice shook. 'You're a sweetheart. Amelia. Thanks so much. The appointment's for eight-thirty, so we'll have to leave a bit after seven. Sorry to get you up so early.'

'Callie, when I start work next week, I'll be up at five most days. I'll be over at the house by seven.'

***

Ben hummed under his breath as he stepped out of the bathroom towelling his hair.

She said yes!

He'd gone really close to not calling Amelia tonight, but he figured nothing ventured, nothing gained. He almost fell over when she'd said yes straight up.

So, he hadn't imagined that look in her eyes a couple of times this afternoon when their gazes had connected over Chilli.

'I take it the puppy school went well.' The dry voice came from behind as he walked up the hall.

'Jeez, Mum, give a man a heart attack. I thought you were in bed. You're up late.'

'I've been on the phone to your father trying to talk him into coming to the garden party but I was wasting my breath. You won't let me down, will you, Ben?'

'No, Mother dear. I gave you my word and I'll be there. It's for a good cause. But knowing what an event you put on, you'll need some more helpers. How about I ask Braden and Kent to help me set up the tables and chairs for you?'

'That would be greatly appreciated. It's the setting up that's the problem. The catering's well under control and I can get some of the young girls in town to come and serve and help clean up.'

'Sounds like it's all under control.' He leaned over and dropped a kiss on the top of his mother's head. 'Good night, mother dear. Don't sit up too late.'

Her eyes widened and she shook her head as he headed toward his room. 'You didn't tell me how the puppy school went.' She chuckled. 'But I guess there's no need to. Someone's in a very good mood.'

'Night, Mum,' he called as he went to close the door. He hesitated and pulled it open and poked his head around. 'Don't go cooking dinner for me tomorrow night. I'll be out.'

'Night, Ben. Sweet dreams.'

The smile stayed on his face after he was in bed and drifting off to sleep.

Chapter 13

Amelia headed over to the house a few minutes before seven. She tapped on the screen door, and Braden was there in an instant opening it for her.

'Thanks so much Amelia, we owe you.'

She smiled. 'My pleasure. The boys and I will have fun.'

'We all had a late night. It was a bit of a tough one, so we put a movie on and watched it until after ten. Petie and Rory are still sound asleep, so make yourself at home here until they wander out. Callie's just having a quick shower and we'll be off. Come into the kitchen and I'll show you where everything is.'

Amelia followed him into the kitchen. Nigel was sitting at the table, a bowl of Weet Bix in front of him. His eyes stayed closed as he spooned the cereal into his mouth, making odd little grunting noises with each mouthful.

She frowned as she looked at Braden, but he chuckled. 'Don't worry, that's Nigel. He eats his brekky like that every day. He's not a morning person. He'll wake up in a minute and turn back into the Nigel we all know and love.' He ruffled his son's hair as he walked over to the long bench under the window. 'Won't you, mate?'

Another grunt.

'Coffee maker is on. Just drop a pod into it when you're ready. Cereal is under here. They all have something different. Toaster, there, and jam and butter in the fridge.'

Callie came in and put her handbag on the table. 'Thanks, Amelia. We should be back by lunchtime. If there's anything you need, just give us a call.'

Five minutes later, she was standing at the window watching the family Landcruiser drive out the gate. The house was silent, only the ticking of the kitchen clock breaking the silence. The wind had picked up overnight and swirling willies of red dust spiralled along the road. It wasn't going to be a very nice day outside. She'd let the boys sleep as long as they wanted.

Chapter 14

The first thing that Ben did on Saturday morning was jump in his car and go around to George Malone's place. He looked around the neat and tidy garden as he walked up to the front door. The green timber door had a frosted glass panel at the top and one of those old-fashioned metal door ringers that you turned to make the bell ring. He tried to turn the ringer but it wouldn't turn; the door looked as though it hadn't been open for a long time. He wiped the rust off his fingers onto the side of his jeans.

Remembering his mother's habit of always welcoming guests at the back door, he stepped off the front porch and headed around the side towards the back of the house, past rose gardens fat with buds.

'Hello,' he called as he spotted an older woman hanging sheets on the old-fashioned clothes prop; pre-Hills Hoist days, it had two timber posts that tilted and lowered the line that she was throwing sheets over.

'Hello there. I'll be with you in a minute.'

As Ben watched, the line flew up on the other side and a strong gust of wind blew the sheet the woman was trying to drape over the wire onto the grass.

'Can I give you a hand?' he said as he walked over.

'That'd be a great help. Thank you. I haven't hung washing on a line like this since I used to stay with my grandmother back in the 1960s!' She laughed as he held the line steady while she retrieved the wet sheet off the grass. When it was draped over the line, she lifted the cane washing basket onto her hip and turned to him. 'What can I do for you?'

'I'm Ben Riley and I spent a lot of time here when I was a boy. Cricket practice.'

'Are you Jenny's boy?'

'I am.' There was no getting away from your country roots in a town this size. When he'd been working in the larger towns, Ben had appreciated the anonymity that had come with living there. It hadn't bothered him at all being referred to as a blow-in.

'I'm Ruth. I guess your mum told you the place was for sale? I bumped into her at IGA yesterday. She said she knew someone who might be interested.'

'Hi Ruth, nice to meet you. I met Fallon and Jon at Easter.'

'You're the singer, aren't you?'

Before he could answer she headed off across the lawn to the house. 'Come on in and we'll have a chat over a cuppa. I'm past due for one, been fighting with that clothesline all morning. But I'm done now. I don't know what possessed me to decide to wash everything in the linen press! It's all going to go to the op shop in the long run anyway.'

Ben held the screen door open for Ruth, and she disappeared into the laundry that was off to one side. He'd been in there a few times as a kid, to get a drink of water on hot afternoons, and the place smelled exactly the same. A damp concrete smell brought the memories rushing back.

Ruth hurried out and gestured to the kitchen. 'Sit down, I put the jug on before I went outside. Now, are you a tea drinker?' She lifted a teapot off the bench top.

'Tea's fine, thank you.'

A few minutes later, Ruth poured tea into a huge mug, and then put a plate of lamingtons on the table. 'Don't tell your mum, but I kept a few of these back from the CWA stall. My husband loves them and I never get a chance to cook when we're home in Brisbane.'

'I'm pleased you did.' He took a sip of burning hot tea and put the mug down on the table. 'So, is Mum right? Is this place for sale? I didn't see a For Sale sign when I came in.'

'The word sure got around,' Ruth said. 'We haven't seen the agent yet, but there's already a bit of interest. I'm surprised actually. I thought it would sit here for months. So, would you like to have a look through?'

'I would. If that's okay before it's on the market?'

'Of course it is. Anyway, from the interest so far, it might not even be advertised. Have another lamington, and you can have a wander while I fight with that old washing machine. Can you believe George still has an old wringer?'

Ben laughed. 'I don't even know what a wringer is.'

'Get away with you. Take your cup of tea and have a look around. Then if you're interested. just let me know and I'll talk to Fallon.'

Ben was careful as he walked up the dark hall carrying the mug of tea. Ruth's welcome had been friendly and she'd made him smile a few times as they'd chatted. He paused and looked into every room. It was obvious that they were cleaning out. Some rooms were empty and some had boxes in the corner. Despite being an old house, it was in good condition, and the rooms were a fair size with high ceilings. He could easily imagine living here.

For a while that was, and then when he moved away, he could rent it. His financial adviser was always telling him to put some of his money into property. There was no sign of Ruth when he rinsed his mug in the kitchen sink. He pushed open the back door and spotted her in a small vegie garden near the back fence.

'Thanks for letting me look around, Ruth. I'll get back to you within a week or so. Do you know how much it will go on the market for yet?'

'No. But I think we'll get it valued in the next few days. Fallon's going down to Charleville tomorrow to do some business, so I'll get her to make some enquiries.'

'Thanks, I'll call in and see you in a week or two if that suits?'

'No rush, Ben. Just let us know if you are seriously interested.'

'I will. Say hello to Fallon for me.'

Chapter 15

Amelia leaned back in the chair and put her hands on the table in front of her. Since she hadn't been working with cattle for a few months her nails had grown and her hands were a lot softer. She'd painted her fingernails tonight—the first time in a couple of years. She'd also gone to a bit more effort with what she wore, and with her hair. As she'd waited for Ben, she'd wondered why she had.

Ben had gone over to the bar to order their meals. He'd had one beer and was changing to Coke now and, Amelia had said no to another wine; deciding one white wine would last her a while.

Being a Saturday night, the pub was busy and full of noise and happy voices, and she relaxed, thinking how nice it was to see more of the town and how it fitted together. A few couples with small children sat out in the beer garden, the restaurant was quite full—most of the customers looked like grey nomies, but she recognised three couples who she'd seen at the Easter events sitting at a large table under the window. Spending most of her time alone or now with Chilli since she had got here—Amelia took an interest in people. She was enjoying the buzz of happiness around her and contentment seeped through her.

She loved this little town.

Chilli was home in the pen with the three pups and had seemed quite happy when she'd left.

Braden and Callie and Nigel had come home just after lunch and Amelia had had the afternoon to herself. She'd checked if Chilli would be okay, and there'd been no problem. When she'd said she was going out for a meal with Ben, Braden and Callie had both smiled.

The effort Amelia had put into getting herself ready to go out had been well worth it from the look on his face when he'd knocked at her door about an hour ago. His eyes were full of admiration and a warm flush went up her neck into her cheeks. No need to pinch her cheeks to get a bit of colour into them tonight.

The trip into town had gone quickly as they chatted the whole way. Amelia had tried hard not to give into her normal nervous habit of talking to fill the silence.

Ben had been full of questions about where she grew up and where she'd travelled, what she was doing here and how she spent her spare time. The conversation was easy as they travelled into town.

As soon as they crossed the road from where Ben had parked, the old man sitting at the table outside the main door of the hotel sat straight.

'Well, hello there, Missy. I've missed you,' he said.

'Gidday, Reg. How have you been?'

'Fair to middling, love. Fair to middling. Come back and have a chat with me later.'

'I will.' Amelia turned to Ben as they walked inside. 'That doesn't sound good. He must have been sick.'

Ben chuckled. 'You'll get to know old Reg. Fair to middling is a good day.'

Amelia got some curious looks as Ben guided her ahead of him. Everyone seemed to know Ben and there were lots of greetings as they crossed to the bistro.

'Gidday, Ben.'

'Good to see you back in town, mate.'

Ben nodded and smiled but didn't stop. The only hello Amelia received was the one from old Reg.

Ben pulled out a chair at the table he'd reserved. 'What would you like to drink?' he asked.

'A small white wine would be great, thanks. If you want to order our meal, I'm happy with a chicken parmi.'

He grinned at her. 'My meal of choice too.

After he walked back to the bar and waited at the counter with his back to her, chatting to the man beside him Amelia took the opportunity to really check Ben out.

For the life of her, she couldn't understand how she had gone from thinking he was a total jerk on their first meeting and really disliking him, to doing a full switch around sitting here thinking what a good-looking man he was, and what a nice guy. She felt totally at ease in his company.

With a slight frown, she tried to ignore that surge of attraction that was making her all warm and fuzzy inside.

Think about what your father would say, she reminded herself.

That'd be right, Amelia. Just rush into everything. Don't think about the consequences, then again you just don't think at all, do you? You just do what you want to.

Dad's criticism stung, even though it was only in her head. She sat up straight and pushed away her thoughts. What consequences could come from having a nice dinner with a very pleasant man? It wasn't as though she was going to hop into bed with him on the way home.

Then again, it had been a long time since she'd hopped into bed with anyone. With a soft sigh, Amelia waited for her new friend to come back.

***

'No gig, tonight, Ben?' Craig Wilson picked up his beer and leaned back on the bar counter.

'No, mate, Kent wanted the weekend off. We've been booked up since the concert out at your place.'

'The word got around, hey. Anyway, it should, I reckon you pair could be the new Keith Urban.'

Ben chuckled. 'Don't think so mate. Sure not going to replace the day job.'

'Good to have you back in town. I'll get you to come out to my place one day when I'm not out on the station. Need a bit of advice. I've seen what Braden's doing with his new accommodation, and I'd like you to have a look at where I'm thinking about building something similar.'

'Sure, how about Wednesday?' Ben swiped his credit card over the EFTPOS as his drinks were charged. Mack, the barman he'd gone to school with handed him a buzzer for their meals.

'Yep, that suits. You'd better go over and give your friend some company. New in town? Although she looks familiar.'

'Yep. She was at the concert at your place.'

'Ah, I remember. The new station hand out at Braden's. I'll have to ask him where he hires. There are a few agencies around these days. None of my blokes are lookers like she is.'

Ben felt uncomfortable discussing Amelia. 'I'll see you Wednesday, Craig.' With a nod, he picked up the drinks and the buzzer and headed back to their table.

He put the drinks on the table carefully and then placed the buzzer in the middle of the table before he sat down.

'It's busy in here tonight. I haven't seen the place humming like this for a few months. Lots of tourists. Good to see.'

'I love this town, so much atmosphere,' Amelia said.

Ben raised his eyebrows. 'Atmosphere? You must have had a very quiet life.'

'Not much happens in the Gulf on the cattle stations and there are no towns like this anywhere close. The only visitors we really had were those who flew in, and then I was away at school most of the time so I can't say it was terribly exciting.'

'I guess that's why you think this is exciting then. How would you go in the big smoke?'

'Oh no.' Amelia shook her head. 'I was in Longreach for a few weeks. Actually, that's where I got Chilli. I'll tell you that story later. I couldn't handle the traffic and the crowds and the noise. So many different people around you. Give me a quiet country town like this any day.'

'We're total opposites,' Ben said with a grin. 'I worked in a Longreach for a while.'

'Inspector?' she asked.

'No, engineer. I did engineering at uni. Came back home for a while and then I got a job in Longreach, and then a promotion to the shire in Charters Towers. I suppose they're not cities, but they're both big enough towns. Then I moved to St George. A bit closer to home.'

'And then you ended up back in Augathella where you grew up. You must have been pleased about that.'

'Not one little bit.' He pulled a face. 'I did my study and became an engineer so I could spread my wings and move somewhere interesting. I applied for a transfer to St George and I wasn't aware they had a reciprocal agreement with Morweh Shire and guess where I ended up? At Augathella as inspector!'

'And you're not happy about it, I'd say?' She raised a quizzical eyebrow.

'My mum is. But how many thirty-something-year-olds still live at home with their mum getting their washing and ironing done?'

'Half your luck. Mind you,' she said with a grin, as a warm shiver ran down Ben's back. 'I wash but

I don't iron. There's not a lot of demand for pressed clothes in the paddock.'

'You're lucky. I've got the ironed shirts and the tie. The boss likes us to look professional.'

'Nothing wrong with that. But you really don't want to be here? That's a shame.'

'It's only a temporary trade,' he said. 'A year or so, but I have the option to choose where I end up. And it won't be here. What about you? Are you on contract?'

'Yes, I am, but I really love this place. I'm looking to settle somewhere and I reckon Augathella might be it.'

'But why Augathella?' he asked, bemused that someone young would really consider moving here.

'It's just the impression I've had. I've only been here a couple of weeks.'

'I thought you'd only been at Kilcoy Station for a few days.'

'No, I arrived just before Easter.' Her grin was cheeky. 'I was at the Easter concert where there was this really good duo playing.'

Ben flushed. 'So, not the time I made a fool of myself with my overreaction to Chilli Girl.'

'No, that was the second time I saw you. I wasn't impressed that the cool singer dude was a jerk.' She hurried on. 'I don't think that now though. Your apology has been very nice, thank you.'

'So, tell me what's contributed to this impression of Augathella that feels so good to you?'

'It just feels right. Kilcoy Station is a great property. I know I haven't been out and looked at most of it yet, but I can tell by looking at the cattle. It's a very well-run property. Jon is taking me out next week to show me what I'll be doing. And as far as the town goes, I've made more friends here than I've made anywhere in such a short time. I've been welcomed to town so warmly.' She gestured outside. 'Even old Reg was extra friendly.'

Ben lowered his voice and looked at her animated expression. 'I'd like to spend more time with you, Amelia. Can you fit in another friend?'

'I can. I'd like to be your friend too.'

Their eyes met and held, and Ben was lost. The spell was broken as the buzzer vibrated on the tabletop between them.

'Guess our dinner is ready,' Ben said looking away and feeling flustered.

What had happened then? He'd never had that strange jolt before. 'Stay there, I'll collect them.'

A couple of minutes later and he'd regained his composure as he carried two meals of chicken parmi back.

'Oh yum, that looks amazing,' Amelia said. 'It's my favourite.'

'I thought you'd be a steak girl.'

She chuckled and her eyes lit up as he sat opposite her and passed over the cutlery. 'Would you believe I don't eat red meat?'

The evening went quickly as they ate and chatted. Amelia watched on quietly as several locals stopped at the table to say hello to him and be introduced to Amelia. Her expression was interested and friendly, and Ben found it hard to take his eyes off her. Eventually, he stood and pushed in his chair.

'It's getting late. Last drinks soon. Are you right to go?'

'Sure,' she replied. He walked around and held her chair as she stood. 'You are a true gentleman, Ben Riley.'

'My mum has always taught me good manners.'

'And that includes picking up a girl and then taking her home?'

'That's exactly right.' It felt right as she slipped her arm through the crook of his elbow as they walked out through the pub.

'Won't be long getting back to Mum,' he thought as Mrs Jenkins smiled at him and nudged her husband in the ribs.

The drive home went quickly as they kept talking. The main house was in darkness when he pulled up outside her donga.

'Thank you, Ben. I'll be right. You go, it's late. I'll just go and check on Chilli.'

'No, I'll come with you and I'll see you to your door. That's what a gentleman does.'

He could see her smile in the darkness as he got out and came around to open the passenger door.

'I could get used to this,' she said as he took her hand and she slid down to the ground.

Ben didn't move as she stood next to him and he kept hold of her hand in the comfortable silence. Eventually, she squeezed his fingers. 'Come on, we'll go over and check if Chilli's happy. If she's settled, I'll leave her there. It's good practice for her for when I have to do overnight work out on the station.'

'Has she been behaving?' Ben asked quietly as they walked over.

Amelia nodded as they walked over to the dog pen behind the shed adjacent to the main house. Chilli came out and licked both their hands, wagging her tail madly as Ben crouched down at the fence.

'Hello, Chill Girl,' he said quietly. There was no sign of the other dogs. Chilli stretched and went back into her kennel at Amelia's command. Amelia turned and beckoned Ben away quietly. Nothing stirred. The night was still, the wind had dropped and the cattle were quiet. The night sky was brilliant, full of diamond stars.

'It's so beautiful, out here, isn't it?' Amelia whispered as they reached her donga. Ben stopped, held her gently and turned her to him.

'It's not the only beautiful thing out here, tonight, Amelia. I hope you don't mind if I kiss you goodnight,' he said as he lowered his head.

Chapter 16

'I don't mind at all,' Amelia whispered. His kiss was beautiful. Softly at first, his lips touched her cheek and then slid slowly to the crease at the edge of her mouth.

'Are you sure?' he murmured.

'I'm sure,' she said quietly, as warm anticipation coursed through her veins. His lips slid gently onto hers and her knees trembled, but Ben's arms held her close as he deepened the kiss. Amelia kept her eyes closed, not wanting it to end.

Finally, he lifted his head and she slowly opened her eyes.

'That was very nice,' she said.

'It was. I have a question for you.' His voice was low and husky.

For a moment she worried that he wanted to stay the night. No matter how good the kiss had been or how much she liked Ben, sex on a first date wasn't something she did.

No matter *how* tempted she was.

'Y . . .e . . .s?' she asked slowly as he turned towards her donga and held her hand.

'I have to go to Charleville tomorrow. I was hoping you'd keep me company. Unless you've got other plans already.'

Amelia shook her head, and his face fell in disappointment.

She squeezed his fingers. 'I have no plans. I'd love to. I haven't been to Charleville yet.'

'Excellent. I just have to make one quick stop and then I'll take you on the tourist trail, and then we'll have lunch at my favourite pub.'

'I hope there's lots of walking involved after that huge dinner I had tonight.'

'There can be. Or I could pack a picnic and we could sit by the river.'

'Or I could buy hamburgers or fish and chips. My turn to shout you. So, tell me about the tourist trail.'

'More red dirt, solar flares, great camping, bilbies, damper, secret WW2 bases, great coffee and star gazing. Wear jeans and walking shoes and I'll show you the sights.'

'All in one day? I'll look forward to it.'

They had reached the bottom step of her donga.

Ben glanced at this watch. 'I guess I'd better get going. Thank you for a great night.'

Again, Amelia was tempted to invite him in for coffee, but she knew if she did, that was giving a signal she wasn't ready for yet. 'Thank you. I'll drive in and meet you in town. What time?'

Ben shook his head. 'No, I'll come and pick you up. My invite, I drive. What about Chilli? Do you want to bring her?'

'I'll check with Callie in the morning to see if she can stay in the pen. I'll get up early and take her for a walk if she stays home.'

'She can come too if you want. We can take her to most places we'll be going. Especially if we have a picnic. Would she be okay in the car for a few minutes now and then?'

'That's very kind of you. And yes, she's used to that.'

'Hey, I love dogs. Even ones that have bitten me.' He laughed and she smiled up at him. 'I'll pick you up at nine. Unless that's too early on a Sunday morning.'

'Nine is good. I'll go over and see Callie early.' Amelia stood on her toes—Ben was tall—and reached up and brushed her lips over his. 'Now get going. I'll see you tomorrow.'

His arms went around her waist and it was a good ten minutes later that Amelia stood watching the tail lights of his four-wheel drive disappear down the road.

She put her fingers to her lips and walked inside, a huge smile on her face. Her feet were almost walking on air.

Or that's what it felt like anyway.

Whoever would have thought it?

Another reason to love Augathella. The only problem was it sounded as though Ben wouldn't be here long.

##

The next morning Amelia was up bright and early. She pulled on her old work clothes and hurried across to the dog pen with Chilli's lead. Chilli had been made so welcome by Callie and the Cartwrights that the least she could do was feed the dogs and clean up the pen.

Chilli came wandering out, stretched and came over for a cuddle.

'Hello, my beautiful girl. Have you been good? I didn't hear a peep out of you all night. Or did I sleep too soundly?' Her sleep had been full of delicious dreams. Each one involved Ben Riley, and she was looking forward to spending more time with him today.

Amelia filled the bowls with kibble and supervised to make sure they all stayed at their own bowl. She filled up the water bowls and then after removing the hessian beds and hanging them on the fence she washed out the concrete pen with the hose. As she turned the tap off, the screen door of the house opened, and Callie came out with a basket of washing on her hip.

'Morning, Amelia,' Callie said glancing across at the pen. 'Oh, thanks so much for doing that. We all slept in.'

'So did the dogs.' Amelia grinned. Happiness was bursting out of her. It was a beautiful day, despite the chill of the autumn wind making her nose cold. 'How did things go yesterday?'

'Really, really good. The new doctor at the hospital, Doctor Higgins, was really thorough and even though he has a brisk and cool manner, Nigel warmed to him straight away. He talked to us with Nigel there first, and then he spent an hour with Nigel. He obviously said the right things, because the first thing Nigel did when he came out was put his arms around and say sorry to me.' Callie blinked. 'I cried.'

'That's progress,' Amelia said. 'I felt so sorry for you yesterday, and poor little Nigel.'

'Yes, as time passes, he's not dealing with Julia's loss as well as Rory and Petie. Dr Higgins has referred him to a child psychologist in Charleville. Thanks so much for looking after the other two. We seem to have imposed on you so much.'

'Not at all. That's what friends are for. Did you need me for anything today?'

'No, of course not. It's Sunday and I know Jon will be here bright and early to take you out to see the station tomorrow. You relax today.' Callie gestured to the dog pen. 'You've already done a day's work there.'

'I was, um, thinking about going to Charleville myself. Ben has to go in and he invited me to go with him.'

Callie looked at her quizzically, and then she smiled when Amelia's cheeks heated.

'Then I guess the dinner date went well?'

'It did. We talked for hours. And I mean we *both* did. I managed not to talk too much for a change. My mum always says I can talk the hind leg off a donkey. Ben is great. He's taking me on the tourist trail of Charleville today.'

'What about Chilli?'

'He said I could bring her.'

'Why don't you leave her here? She's no trouble and the pups and the boys love her.'

'Would that really be all right? I hate imposing. I really do.'

'Of course, it's okay! Now you go and get ready. Leave Chilli's lead here. The boys can take her for a walk later. And don't rush home, although make sure you watch out for roos if you're home after dark. They were pretty bad last night.'

'Ben's coming out to pick me up. And drop me home.'

Callie's eyebrows rose. 'Wow, I'm impressed. He must be smitten. He's a really nice guy.'

'He is.' Amelia felt her cheeks heat again. 'Anyway, we won't be too late because I have an early start tomorrow. Jon said we'd be heading out at six.'

'Okay, you have a good day. Oh, and while I think of it, another station hand will be moving into the second donga today, so don't worry if you see a light there. His name's Charlie Cavanagh. One of our regulars. He usually camps out in a swag, but he's finally admitted he's too old to sleep on the ground.'

'Okay, thanks. I wondered if there was someone there.'

'Soon. He's a real character. Now go make yourself beautiful, girlfriend!'

Amelia crouched down and gave Chilli Girl a pat and a hug as Callie headed to the clothesline. 'You be a good girl, and I'll see you this afternoon.'

***

Ben wandered out to the kitchen still in his PJs and covered a yawn with the back of his hand.

'Morning, Mum,' he said.

'Morning, sweetheart. You look tired. You had a late night last night, didn't you?'

'I did and I've got to head off to Charleville this morning. What are your plans for the day?'

'I'm spending the whole day in the garden. I've got a lot of pruning to do and I want to mulch the rose garden and I'd like to—'

'Do you need your car today?' Ben interrupted. He knew Mum could talk forever about what her plans were in the garden.

'No, I don't have any intentions of going anywhere today. Do you want to borrow it?'

'I do. I'm off to Charleville. Billy Hanna called me last week. He's got a new guitar in stock and I said I couldn't get down through the week so he's taken it home and I said I'd call in today.'

'So, you need my car to bring home a new guitar? If you buy it.'

'Not exactly. I'm . . .ah . . . taking someone with me for the drive.' He tried to keep a casual tone but Mum honed right in.

'Would that be the pretty girl you had dinner with at the hotel last night?'

Ben rolled his eyes. 'God, Mum, this is why I hate living in Augathella. Nothing's private. You can't even take a leak without someone knowing.'

'No need to be crude. It's one of the reasons you should love living in a town like this. People like you, people care about you, and people are interested in what you do. Everyone is so pleased to see you back in town and everyone is saying what a great job you're doing on the shire.

'Well, it would be nice to have somewhere different to go for dinner and not have the whole town know the next morning where you've been and what you ate.'

'And how was the chicken parmi?' Jenny chuckled and put her hands up. 'And no. No one told me what you had for dinner. I just know you well, my boy. Mind you, I remember when I was teaching at the high school and some of the kids had after-school jobs. I did hate that everybody in town knew what you and your father and I were having for dinner every night when I used to go to IGA on the way home.'

'Then you know exactly what I'm saying.'

'I do, but don't change the subject. Tell me who you were having dinner with. From all accounts, she's very pretty.'

'You're incorrigible, Mum. She's a new station hand out at Braden's property. I met her a week or so ago when I was out there looking at the concrete for his new dongas

'Oh, she was the one whose dog bit you and you did the puppy school with on Friday night. Quick work, son. Friday night puppy school Saturday night dinner, Sunday Charleville. Hmmm.'

'That's enough hmming from you Mum. We're simply friends and I thought she might like to see Charleville while I'm down there. There's lots to see. I haven't been to the World War II site yet.'

'That's fine, take my car. I won't need it but you might like to give it a bit of a sweep out first because I brought home some fertiliser the other day and it spilt in the backseat. There's a bit of a smell in there.'

'In your Audi? You put chook poo in the Audi? For goodness' sake, Mum, next time put it in the boot or ask me and I'll pick it up in my ute.'

'It's okay. It'll clean. I'll dig out some air freshener So is she coming in and meeting you here? I'd better get out of my dressing gown. A mother never wants to meet her son's—'

'Mum!'

'I was going to say meet her son's friends in her dressing gown.' But her smile was devious.

'No. I'm going to take my ute out and pick her up at Kilcoy Station and then we'll call in here and swap cars over. I guess if you're home, you'd like to meet Amelia. She likes Augathella.'

'An excellent influence on you. And I'd love to meet her. That's what this town needs. More young blood moving in. Have you heard about the new young couple in town with the organic vegie crops?'

'I have.' Ben was relieved she'd finally got off the subject of meeting Amelia.

'One thing I will say if you are interested in George Malone's house, I'd get a move on. There are a few newbies in town. There might be a bit of interest.'

'I'll think about it.' He wasn't going to let on he'd already looked at the house but it seemed that nugget of news hadn't got back to Mum yet. That was a first.

She tipped her head to one side. 'First time I've known you to take someone out for quite a long time.'

'Mum, you've got no idea what I've been doing while I've been in Longreach and Charters Towers and St George.'

'I know. That's why it's so good to have you home and I do know what's happening.' She giggled, more like a teenager than a fifty-five-year-old. 'What are you going to wear today? Your dark brown long-sleeved shirt is ironed. It brings out the colour of your eyes. You've got your father's eyes. They always sucked me in when we were courting.'

'Mum! I am not courting! And if I was, I wouldn't tell you. Now get out in that garden, Mother. I'm going to have a shower.' Ben ruffled her hair on his way out as she sat at the kitchen table drinking her cup of tea.

Chapter 17

'Your mum's lovely.'

Ben smiled as they turned onto the highway towards Charleville.

'She was certainly on her best behaviour. I don't think she was game to be anything else,' he chuckled.

'Beautiful garden. I envy her. It's one thing I want to do. I'd love to have a yard where I can grow my flowers.'

'You'd like to settle one day?'

'I would. I'd love to have my own place with a bit of land. I could bring my horse down. I do miss her.'

For some reason, Amelia didn't want to say that she was looking at a place in Augathella because she knew how much Ben wanted to get out; she worried that he would judge her. That she was rushing in before she really knew the town, or before she had a permanent job, not just a contract. He didn't need to know that money wasn't an issue for her.

'Me too. I'd like to have my own place. I just don't know where yet. I certainly don't want to be living with my parents for the rest of my life.' He pulled a face and she grinned at him.

'Tell me where we're going today,' she said. 'What this tourist trail tour is.'

'Well, if you don't mind the first thing, I have to do is to call in and see a mate and pick up a guitar I've bought.'

'No problem at all. I'm in your hands.' The look he gave her was cheeky.

'Nice,' he said.

'Don't be rude,' Amelia said but her smile stayed.

'Then it's your choice. You tell me what you'd like to do. There are a lot of things to see. Are you into stars?'

'What sort of stars? Movie stars or sky stars? Or astrology stars? I had my tarot cards read at the van park in Longreach.'

The banter continued between them for the next hour or so and in the end, they decided to begin the tour at the Cosmos Centre after Ben had picked up his guitar.

Amelia sat in the car and sent her weekly text home while she waited; she'd forgotten to do it earlier. She shook her head with a grin. She'd been too excited waiting for Ben to come and collect her for their day out. She called home only on rare occasions, and her parents never rang her.

Thank goodness for text messages.

Hi Mum and Dad. Hope all is well. I'm good. I'm starting work at Kilcoy Station tomorrow, it's a good spread Dad. Might get home to collect Brinny one day soon. I miss my girl. You'd love the fat and shiny cattle here. Love Amelia.

A door closed and she watched Ben as he came out of the house carefully carrying a guitar case. He placed it almost reverently on the back seat.

'She's a beauty. Emerald green and she sings. Can't wait to play her at our next gig.'

'A singing guitar? I've never seen one of them,' she teased. 'You'll have to tell me where it is. I'd love to hear you both again.'

'We're up at Tambo at the pub next weekend. Sunday afternoon gig.'

'I'll see if I'm working. How far is it?'

'About an hour north,' he said. 'You could come with me if you wanted.'

'I'll see what happens. I can't go leaving Chilli all the time. That's not why I got her.'

'Dogs are allowed at the pub there.'

'I'll see.'

'Okay.'

Ben obviously picked up not to push her.

'I really enjoyed listening to you and Kent performing at the Easter concert. You did sing a little bit that night, didn't you?'

'Sometimes, but Kent's the one with the voice. I just love to play guitar.'

'Do you play any other instruments?'

'Yeah, the piano, and I've got a drum set back in the garage at home. What about you?'

'I love listening to music but I'm pretty much tone deaf. Can't sing, don't play any instruments, unless you count the recorder at school. The teachers used to despair of me at boarding school. I couldn't even play that well.'

'Boarding school? High school?'

'No. From when I was ten.'

'Was that hard?'

'Sure was. I missed being out on the land. And I missed my horse.'

He glanced at her and she realised she hadn't said anything about her family.

'Oh, and my brothers, of course.'

Amelia was pleased when he changed the subject.

'Any other hobbies?'

'Riding. I know that's work, but it's also a passion of mine. I so miss my horse. I left Brinny at home. It'll be good to be on horseback tomorrow. When I do settle somewhere I'll bring her down. She smiled and looked out of the car. 'Are we going to sit and chat all day or are we going to see the stars now?'

'We are.' Ben started the Audi and pulled out onto the road. 'That's the railway station. We can come back here later for the bilby show. I rang up and checked what time it was on. If you still want to go, that is.'

'I do. I tell you what though. I'd love a coffee. Is there a café where we're going?'

'I'm not sure, but there are a few good coffee places in town. You're a woman after my own heart. I love a good coffee. Plus, I'm hungry.'

Amelia nodded. 'I should be embarrassed to admit it, but so am I. Coffee and cake sound good to me.'

'Well, that's at least one thing we have in common,' Ben said. 'And you've got a big week of work ahead, I guess.'

'I do. What about you?'

'I've got a bit of travelling this week. I'll be out at Kilcoy for a meeting with Braden sometime, but I guess you'll be out on the station.'

'Text me and let me know when you'll be there. I might be able to give you a coffee if it's late in the day.' She put on a smug smile. 'I have a very good coffeemaker for coffee snobs.'

'I will. Have you got next weekend off? And what about Friday night for Chilli's puppy class?'

'I'll know more tomorrow.' She looked down as Ben reached over and touched her hand briefly.

'Stay in touch through the week?'

'If you'd like me to.'

'I would,' he said as he turned into an area that looked like the main business centre. He took a right and parked outside an old house that had been turned into a historical museum.

'Good.'

'You could be sorry you asked that. You might find me totally painful today after you show me around.'

'I don't think that's a possibility. I'm getting to know you. And I like what I see.'

Chapter 18

The next week flew past with only one minor incident, but that solved the mystery of poor Chilli's initial incident with Ben. After two days out on horseback with Jon, Amelia spent Wednesday in the main shed with him, learning more about the property and her role over the next few months. Charlie, the other new arrival had gone to join the team mustering in the far paddocks. Amelia was pleased that to begin with she would be mostly on horseback, mustering and looking after steers that needed attention and would be held in a paddock not far from the homestead.

When Ben texted on Wednesday to say he would be calling in to see Braden at about four-thirty, she was able to respond she would be home and would have the coffee on.

Callie was in the house garden when Amelia walked back from the shed just after three.

'Hey,' she called out. 'How's your week been, Amelia? You've had a couple of long days.'

'I have but I've loved every minute of it. Kilcoy Station is so well run.'

Callie smiled. 'I'm more up to date with education than agriculture or cattle work but I'm pleased you're happy.'

'I have a huge favour to ask, but feel free to say no.'

'What can I do for you?

Amelia looked around. 'The boys aren't home from school yet?'

'No. It's my other day at home, and Braden took them in. He had to go down to Charleville for the day but he's at the school getting them now. He's not long called. They're coming straight home because he's got a meeting here with Ben around four. Why? What's up?'

'I really hope I'm not overstepping, but Ben's going to have a coffee with me, and I haven't been shopping. I don't even have a dry biscuit in the donga. Would you mind if I baked a cake in your kitchen and I'll just take a couple of slices and the boys can have the rest for afternoon tea? I'll pay for the ingredients.'

'Of course, you can. And you're not paying for anything. Come in now and we'll have a cuppa while you get started.'

'I'll just race back and have a wash and get changed.'

Callie grinned. 'I'm sure Ben will like you just the way you are.'

Amelia grinned back. 'Give me five.' She hurried to her donga, had a quick wash, got rid of the cattle smell, and slipped into a pair of clean jeans and a plain T-shirt She didn't want to look like she'd made too much of an effort.

Half an hour later, she and Callie were sitting on the veranda with a coffee and the aroma of the sultana cake baking in the oven drifting out through the doorway. Chilli and the three pups were playing chase on the lawn inside the house fence.

'I meant to ask you before. Are you free on Saturday night?' Callie asked. 'Sophie called me to invite us all to dinner. Kent was going to ask Ben, but they weren't sure whether you pair were a couple or what. So, she asked me to invite you, and he's going to invite Ben.'

Amelia flushed. 'Um, we get on well, and we enjoy each other's company. The day we spent in Charleville was great and we ended up having a late one because Ben took me to the Corones Hotel for an early dinner. I'm going to Tambo with him and Kent on Sunday, but Saturday's free.'

'Sounds pretty good to me,' Callie said.

'But we're just friends,' Amelia insisted.

'So far.' Callie winked. 'Look there's a car coming. Too soon for Braden. It must be Ben. I'll go and check that sultana cake for you.'

Amelia stood and went to the gate yard so Ben would see she was at the house.

He waved and parked the shire ute over near the shed. She waited until he came across, and Chilli ran over to her for a pat.

She crouched down and hugged her dog. 'You've been such a good girl.' She was rewarded with a wet lick on her cheek. They'd been practising the instructions that Ben had taught them last Friday night. She laughed as the other three pups came over and sat when she commanded them to while Ben stood at the gate.

He smiled at her and a warm fuzzy feeling ran through her. His eyes stayed on hers as he lifted the latch.

Would he kiss her hello? Or was it too public?

Or were they just friends?

Ben looked down as Chilli began to creep towards the gate, a low growl emanating from her throat.

'Chilli!' Amelia commanded. 'Sit. Now!'

She leaned forward to hold Chilli's collar, but her dog took off before she could grab her.

Ben stood stock still as Chill bounded towards him, barking, and the bark held a menace. Amelia dived after her and finally caught her just before she reached the gate, her growl deepening and her teeth bared.

'Ben, shut the gate, quick,' she yelled as she tried to hold Chilli back.

Finally, the angry dog settled once Ben was behind the gate again. Amelia frowned as she looked down at her usually docile dog.

She looked up at Ben, and he shrugged, and then she looked back down at Chilli who had started to whimper.

Crouching down, she held the pup's chin firmly in her hand. 'What is it, sweetie? What's wrong?'

Callie opened the door and walked down the steps. 'Hi, Ben, come on in. Cake's ready, Amelia.'

'I'll be there in a minute. Thanks,' Ben called back.

Amelia bit her lip. Chilli was looking at Ben and shaking.

Callie came over to the gate. 'What's wrong?'

'Chilli tried to go for Ben again.'

'But she's been okay with him since last week, hasn't she?'

'She has. She loved him at puppy school last week.'

'What's happened?'

'Nothing.' Amelia looked up at Ben, her heart breaking. If Chilli didn't like Ben, she couldn't keep seeing him. She'd already been through one lot of trauma and been abandoned. Amelia wouldn't do that to her again.

'Can you hold her for me please? I'll go over and talk to Ben.' She handed the lead to Callie. But hold her tight. She's strong.'

As she handed the lead to Callie, Ben called her name.

'Amelia, wait. I think I know what the problem is. Let me try something.'

She and Callie stood back and watched as Ben turned his back for a minute.

When he turned around, Chilli Girl looked up and wagged her tail. He hadn't moved or spoken and hadn't greeted her. Amelia looked on in amazement.

It was as much as if she was saying, 'Ben, it's you!'

Ben opened the gate and with a happy woof, Chilli ran over to him and as he crouched down, Amelia could see what he'd done.

'Well, will you look at that,' she said to Callie.

He'd taken his tie off, and his name tag, and rolled up his long sleeves. The official look had gone and now he just looked like Ben.

Amelia walked over to the gate and stood beside them. Without paying any regard to Callie, he leaned over and kissed Amelia on the lips.

'Hello.'

'Hello, you,' she said against his warm mouth.

Callie was smiling when they turned to her.

'I know what we have to work on with Chilli,' Ben said. 'The authority look. She's obviously been hurt by someone looking official.'

'Can you work with her on that?' Amelia asked anxiously.

'I can but it will mean spending a lot more time with Chilli and her owner.'

'Excellent. Good work, Ben! Now that's sorted do you want cake and coffee here or over at Amelia's place?' Callie said.

Amelia looked at Ben, and Ben looked at Callie.

'Do you have real coffee, Callie? I know Amelia's fussy.'

'I know who's fussy,' she said. 'And despite that I made you a cake!'

'I'll go and grind the beans and leave you two to argue,' Callie said with a wide grin. 'But be quick because I can see the dust from Braden's car. You'll get no peace once the boys are home.'

Ben opened his arms and Amelia stepped into them.

And there wasn't one peep out of Chilli Girl.

Chapter 19

Saturday night

As usual Ben had insisted on driving out to Kilcoy Station to pick Amelia up for the dinner at the pub on Saturday night. Sophie and Kent had organised the dinner, and apparently, a large group was going.

Ruth Malone was minding the boys so Callie and Braden could have a night out. They left for town before Ben arrived.

Amelia was strangely nervous; she'd tried to chase the feeling away as she'd walked back from the dog pen where Chilli had settled happily for the night.

Why did she feel so strange?

Wasn't this what she'd wanted?

To become part of a community?

She fussed about what to wear and fiddled with her hair. Tying it back, leaving it loose and then tying it up again.

When she heard Ben's ute pull up outside, she ran to the mirror and a pale face looked back at her. She pinched her cheeks until they had some colour, smoothed her hand down her skirt, and slipped her knee-length boots on over her tights.

Had she fallen into this relationship too quickly? Was she doing everything that Dad always said she did? Rushed in, no thought?

Like she had when she had rescued Chilli Girl? Like she had when she'd seen the job at Kilcoy Station and applied without thinking twice?

At least she'd pulled back on buying the Malone house. That would have been too much of a rush with the financial outlay. So, see, Dad, she could be sensible.

But with Ben, all sense flew out the window.

She'd lost it when Ben had kissed her the first time.

There had been many kisses since then, but that's where they'd left it for the time being. But she knew if Ben had had his own place, things would have moved much more quickly.

Had she got in too deep too fast?

Amelia put a shaking hand to her face as his footsteps on the stairs shook the flimsy donga. She opened the door and a long wolf whistle came from the verandah of the other donga.

Charlie Cavanagh was out there having a smoke. 'Looking good, girlie. Sorry, Ben,' he chuckled. 'Just admiring, not stepping on your toes, mate.'

Ben gave him a wave and held his other hand out to Amelia.

'You look drop-dead gorgeous.' His dark eyes snagged hers and she drew a quick breath.

She held her breath at his expression, and her doubts fled in an instant. 'You don't look too bad yourself,' she said reaching up to kiss him and that brought another whistle from Charlie.

Ben put his arm around her. 'Hurry up and get in the car. That westerly wind has come early.'

She climbed into the warmth of the cabin, and Ben hurried around and opened his door. Once in, he sat there for a moment and didn't start the car.

'What's wrong?' she asked.

'I wanted to tell you something. A couple of things actually. Before we get to the pub and the grapevine kicks into gear.'

She drew another quick breath. 'You're leaving town?'

Ben stared at her for a long minute. 'Do you think I could?' he finally said.

'I know you want to.'

'I wanted to leave the life I had here. But I've grown to love it here a lot more in the last few weeks. Since a certain dog tried to bite me.'

'But?'

'But I've also met someone I want to get to know a lot better. I'm not going to rush you,

Amelia. We have all the time in the world to explore where this is taking us.'

'But you hate living at home. And you don't like your job.'

'I do like my job.' His expression held a lot of satisfaction. 'My new job. I didn't tell you I applied for another one. Meet the new shire engineer for Morweh Council. Not a new job, but I was asked if I was interested in a promotion. I got the nod today.'

'So, you're moving to Charleville?'

'No, I'm moving out of home, but not that far. A little bit closer to Charleville.' He smiled at her. 'About a kilometre closer.'

'Stop teasing me. Where to?'

He folded his arms and looked very satisfied. 'I've bought a house. It has land and it could do with a horse there if you know anyone who's looking for a place to leave their horse.'

'Oh, my goodness,' she exclaimed. 'Did you buy George Malone's house?'

His face was a picture. 'Do you know George? How did you know his house was for sale?'

'Because I looked through it and fell in love with it, and thought about buying it myself!'

'So, you wouldn't mind living on the edge of town. Maybe one day?'

'If the right offer was made one day, I'd certainly consider it. Like you said, Ben, we have all the time in the world.'

It was quite a while before Ben drove them into town.

Epilogue

The pub

Braden put his arm around Callie's shoulder and he looked around, satisfied. His little sister, Sophie, caught his eye and her smile was wide as she looked back at him. Her fiancé, Kent, was deep in conversation with Jon Ingram, and Fallon was sitting at the end of the table, one hand on her very pregnant stomach. Kent's sister, Jacinta, was sitting beside Sophie's best friend, Kimberly, and a couple of their teacher friends from the primary school were at the other end of the table with their partners, all local cattlemen Braden had worked with.

The queue at the bistro was growing quickly and Callie leaned into him. 'Do you think we should wait for Ben and Amelia, or should we order?'

Braden gestured to the door. 'Here they are now. I'd say Ben took Amelia for a drive to show her what he's bought.'

'Has he got a new car?'

'Nope. He's bought a house. George Malone's place. Ruth and her husband have finished here and they're going back to Brisbane for a couple of months until the baby's born.'

Callie elbowed him in the ribs. 'How come I work in town but you know more gossip than I do?'

'Because I'm a local.' He pressed his lips close to her ear.' And you could be too, if you agreed to set a wedding date.'

He felt Callie's withdrawal and a chill ran through him. He just hoped it wasn't a premonition.

'Don't push, Bray. I agreed to stay engaged, but we won't get married until we're sure it's the right thing for the boys.'

'I'm sorry, sweetheart. I love you, and I want you to be my wife.'

'And I've said yes, but when Nigel's better.'

Kent stood up and dinged a spoon on the side of his beer glass. It was barely heard over the noise in the bistro, so he put two fingers to his mouth and whistled.

There was instant silence, not only at their table but in the whole bistro.

'Ssh everyone, Kent's gonna sing us a song, came a quavering voice from the bar.

'I'll sing you a song, Reggie,' he replied with a laugh. 'Thanks for coming, everyone. Sophie and I just wanted to say a few words while we had you all together, and before we all start eating.'

Sophie stood up and took Kent's hand and satisfaction filled Braden. His sister was settled, and she had a good man.

'Thanks, everyone,' Sophie echoed Kent's words. 'Kent and I have set a wedding date.'

Cheers and clapping filled the room, and she waited for the noise to subside before she continued. 'September three, the first Saturday in spring. And three lovely ladies have agreed to be my bridesmaids. Stand up, girls!'

Kimberly Riordan was the first to stand and another cheer went up. Kent's sister, Jacinta stood slowly, her cheeks flushed with embarrassment. Braden felt sorry for her; where Kent was an outgoing performer, Jacinta was an introvert.

Another round of clapping ensued, and Braden was surprised when Callie lifted his arm and she too stood. She grinned down at him and he grinned back.

'Well, I never,' he said.

'A bridesmaid, my dear, not a matron of honour,' she whispered.

'I'll bring you round,' he said.

Things had been tough lately. Since Nigel's meltdown, Callie had moved into the spare room, and he worried that it was the start of a division between them.

The new doctor, Harry Higgins, had assured him that it was a wise move, to give Nigel time to adjust to Callie being their step mum. Braden was torn; he wanted the best for Nigel, but he also didn't want to let Callie go.

If he'd been a stronger man when Julia had died and kept the boys, maybe Nigel would have been better.

'Patience, my darling.' Callie's lips brushing across his cheek made him feel a little better. 'I'll go and order for us. You grab yourself another beer.'

At least Callie had agreed to stay in a room at the pub tonight and the boys were sleeping over at the Malone's house.

'The usual steak with mushroom sauce?' she asked. 'And garlic bread?'

'You know me well.'

As Callie walked across to the counter with Sophie, Braden saw Kent half-rise in his chair, his face leached of all colour. He was staring at the door that led out to the street.

Braden turned with a frown and for a moment his heart stopped.

Julia?

And then sense kicked in. Julia was in the local cemetery, and this woman was a lot taller than his wife had been. But the shock of seeing a face almost identical to Julia's had him standing without even thinking about it.

He gripped the back of his chair as she walked over to him.

'Hello, Braden.' Her tone was cold and her accent plummy, and he suddenly realised who it was.

'Laura,' he whispered.

'Yes, Braden. It looks like all I've heard is true. You and your new woman are out drinking while those three motherless boys are where?' She looked around. 'Out in the beer garden? Or home alone? Nothing would surprise me from you.'

Braden took her arm and tried to lead her outside before she made a scene. Julia had always told him what a loose cannon his sister-in-law was, and despite being married to Julia for almost seven years, he'd never met Laura Adnum. As far as he'd known she still lived in the UK.

What on earth was she doing here in Augathella?

THE END

UNTIL THE NEXT STORY...

Callie, Fallon, Sophie, and Amelia's stories continue in *Outback Dawn* as we learn more about those who live in the district and those who come for a visit. Will the charms of Augathella keep them there?

Will Braden and Callie tie the knot?
When is Fallon's baby going to arrive?
Will Sophie and Kent's wedding be the one the district is waiting for?
Will Amelia stay at Kilcoy Station or will Ben entice her into town?

Coming in September 2022

When Laura Adnum, sister-in-law of Braden Cartwright, arrives unexpectedly in Augathella to visit the three sons of her deceased sister, Julia, it seems she is there to cause trouble; Laura is not impressed that Braden is planning to marry Callie Young.

Newly-appointed local doctor, Harry Higgins, is surprised when Laura insists on visiting him to check that the care of her three nephews is adequate. Harry has his own demons and has come to Augathella for peace and a quiet life. Harry is suspicious of Laura's motives. Why has she suddenly decided to visit three nephews she has never met? He tries to ignore his instant attraction to this enigmatic woman.

What secrets does each of them hold, and can they each find peace through love?

Outback Dawn: click here

ANNIE SEATON

The Augathella Girls series.

Book 1: Outback Roads -The Nanny

Book 2: Outback Sky – The Pilot

Book 3: Outback Escape – The Sister

Book 4: Outback Winds – The Jillaroo

Book 5: Outback Dawn – The Visitor

Book 6: Outback Moonlight – The Rogue

Book 7: Outback Dust – The Drifter

Book 8: Outback Hope – The Farmer

If you would like to stay up to date with Annie's releases, subscribe to her newsletter here:

http://www.annieseaton.net

OTHER BOOKS from ANNIE

Whitsunday Dawn
Undara
Osprey Reef
East of Alice (November 2022)

Porter Sisters Series

Kakadu Sunset

Daintree

Diamond Sky

Hidden Valley

Larapinta

Pentecost Island Series

Pippa

Eliza

Nell

Tamsin

Evie

Cherry

Odessa

Outback Wind

Sienna

Tess

Isla

The Augathella Girls Series (2022)

Outback Roads

Outback Skies

Outback Escape

Outback Winds

Outback Dawn

Outback Moonlight

Outback Dust

Outback Hope

Sunshine Coast Series

Waiting for Ana

The Trouble with Jack

Healing His Heart

Sunshine Coast Boxed Set

ANNIE SEATON

The Richards Brothers Series

The Trouble with Paradise

Marry in Haste

Outback Sunrise

Richards Bothers Boxed Set

Bondi Beach Love Series

Beach House

Beach Music

Beach Walk

Beach Dreams

The House on the Hill

Second Chance Bay Series

Her Outback Playboy

Her Outback Protector

Her Outback Haven

Her Outback Paradise

The McDougalls of Second Chance Bay   Boxed Set

OUTBACK WIND

Love Across Time Series

Come Back to Me

Follow Me

Finding Home

The Threads that Bind

Love Across Time Boxed Set

Others

Deadly Secrets

Adventures in Time

Silver Valley Witch

The Emerald Necklace

Worth the Wait

Ten Days in Paradise

Her Christmas Star

An Aussie Christmas Duo

Secrets of River Cottage (November 22)

About the Author

Annie lives in Australia, on the beautiful north coast of New South Wales. She sits in her writing chair and looks out over the tranquil Pacific Ocean.

She writes contemporary romance and loves telling stories that always have a happily ever after. She lives with her very own hero of many years and they share their home with Toby, the naughtiest dog in the universe, and Barney, the ragdoll puss, who hides when the four grandchildren come to visit.

Stay up to date with her latest releases at her website: http://www.annieseaton.net

Printed in Great Britain
by Amazon